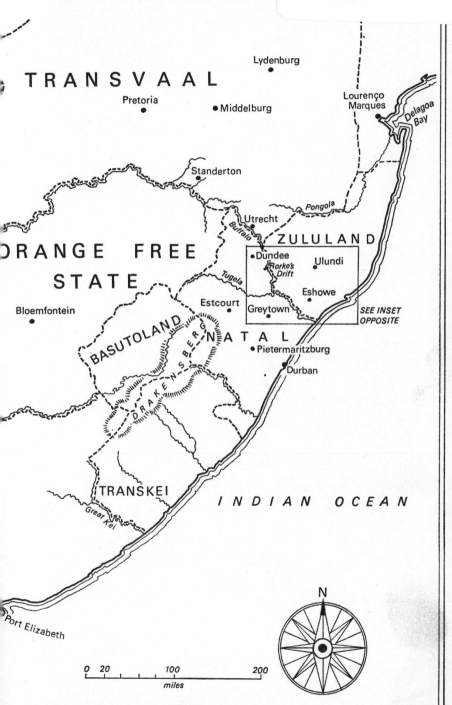

SOUTH AFRICA at the time

D1582036

TRANSVAAL

Lydenburg

Pretoria

Middelburg

Lourenço
Marques

Delagoa
Bay

Standerton

Pongola

Utrecht

Buffalo

ZULULAND

ORANGE FREE
STATE

Dundee

Rorke's
Drift

Ulundi

Tugela

Eshowe

Bloemfontein

Estcourt

Greytown

SEE INSET
OPPOSITE

BASUTOLAND

DRAKENSBERG

NATAL

Pietermaritzburg

Durban

TRANSKEI

INDIAN   OCEAN

Great Kei

N

Port Elizabeth

0   20   100   200
            miles

W. T. GRAHAM,
   34 BIDDALL DRIVE,
      MANCHESTER.
   M23 8PF.

January, 1977.

RORKE'S DRIFT

RORKE'S DRIFT

A Victorian Epic

by

Michael Glover

LEO COOPER · LONDON

For
STEPHANIE
With love

First published in Great Britain 1975 by
LEO COOPER LTD
196 Shaftesbury Avenue, London WC2

Copyright © 1975 by Michael Glover

ISBN 0 85052 182 3

Printed in Great Britain by
the Barleyman Press, Bristol

Contents

Illustrations

The author and publishers would like to thank the following
for permission to reproduce copyright illustrations: The
Mansell Collection, nos 1, 2, 3, 4, 6 and 16; The Regimental
Museum, The South Wales Borderers, nos 12, 13, 14 and 15;
C. Wilkinson-Latham, nos 7, 8, 9 and 10; the Radio Times
Hulton Picture Library, no 11, and The Society for Army
Historical Research, no 5.

Preface

The defence of Rorke's Drift is something of a phenomenon. About a hundred fit men, well armed and behind improvised but effective fortification, defeated a force thirty or forty times as large but armed with primitive weapons. It would have been understandable that the battle would have become an epic if, like the three hundred at Thermopylae, the defenders had all died. In fact they survived with astonishingly few casualties. They were exceedingly brave men (as were their assailants) but outstanding bravery is almost commonplace in British military history. There were plenty of feats of quite astonishing courage in most of our nineteenth century wars but, apart from major actions like Waterloo and Balaklava, very few are widely remembered. Even today Rorke's Drift is remembered, but who except specialist historians recall the equally brave men who defended the Maya Pass on 25 July, 1813, or the stand of the Corps of Guides at Kabul, eights months after Rorke's Drift? In no other action has the Victoria Cross been awarded to one in twelve of those present and never, as far as I can trace, have the thanks of the House of Commons been voted to two subalterns for the same battle. It detracts nothing from the bravery and steadiness of Chard, Bromhead and their men to say that their feat attracted more attention than would normally have been the case.

The explanation lies in the fact that it was in the interest of two influential groups—the government and the army reformers—to draw attention away from their failings or supposed failings. The government, and half a century of previous governments, had neglected South Africa. Very properly they had made their main interest the security of the harbours round the Cape but, Whig or Tory, Conservative or Liberal, they had paid insufficient and intermittent attention to the problems which relentlessly built up in the hinterland. The army reformers, headed by Wolseley, had rebuilt the army on lines which were open to much just, and floods of unjust, criticism. The interests of government and reformers met when the army suffered an unexpected defeat at Isandhlwana. Having erased Bergen-op-Zoom and New Orleans from their collective memories, the public had, for sixty-one years, expected the same invincibility from their army that they assumed for the Royal Navy. To be defeated by a pack of naked barbarians made the humiliation all the greater. Rorke's Drift was the salve for wounded national pride. It drew attention away from many sins of omission and commission.

Since 1936 there has been a steady stream of books about the Zulu war of which Sir Reginald Coupland's *Zulu Battle Piece* and Donald R. Morris's *The Washing of the Spears* have been the most notable. It is hard to say why the war of 1879 has attracted so much attention. There had been seven earlier 'Kaffir' wars in South Africa since the British took over the Cape. There was a steady stream of other colonial campaigns throughout the century but none of these has attracted a tenth of the attention of the campaign against Cetshwayo. It is tempting to think that the fascination lies in the fact that it included a major defeat for the British but, if that is so, it can be asked why a similar interest has not built up round the equally disastrous battle of Maiwand which was fought and lost only eighteen months later in Afghanistan.

In retelling the story of Rorke's Drift I have tried to put the battle in its British setting rather than in the strictly South African context in which it is usually seen. While the breaking of the Zulu power had great significance to the settlers, British and Boer, in South Africa, to the British people it was merely another step in the costly and unwanted escalation of their commitments at the Cape. Imperialism is a dirty word today but those who condemn it seldom realize that, at any rate in the British case, it was a reluctant process, most of all in South Africa which, even at the time of the Zulu war, seemed to offer little or nothing in the way of commercial return for the lives and money expended in acquiring it. When the mineral wealth of Kimberley and the Rand was appreciated in Britain, the attitude to South Africa changed but in 1879 the general view was that it consisted of nothing but 'hundreds of miles of sand ... defying all hopes of improvement'. This made a defeat there all the more distressing and it was the more essential to fix public attention on the epic of Rorke's Drift.

For help in writing this book I would particularly like to thank Lieutenant Colonel F. T. Stear, R.E., the Librarian and Secretary of the Royal Engineers Historical Society, Brigadier John Stephenson, Mr R. A. Brown of the University of Natal Library, Mr Maurice Brown, Mr Timothy Owen and, for a service outside his usual duties as the landlord of the King's Head, France Lynch, Mr Leslie Rea. I must also thank my daughter Stephanie for quantities of assistance and, most of all, my wife, whose long-term interest in the Zulu war sustained me almost as much as she does in so many other ways.

CHAPTER 1

Afternoon on the Buffalo

At Rorke's Drift the Buffalo river is more than a hundred yards wide. Upstream and down it is rock-strewn and dangerous with only rare and difficult fords. At the Drift it is smooth bottomed and Jim Rorke, a trader who died in 1875, had cut away the banks so that horsemen and wagons could cross with ease when the river was low. For the pedestrian it was not a good ford. The water was chest high to a tall man and on 22 January, 1879, it was running at seven miles an hour. On that day, however, there was no need to wade the stream. Two large iron ponts, flat-bottomed square-ended boats, each large enough to accommodate eighty men, had been hauled across country in sections by teams of sixteen oxen and assembled on the river bank. For ten days they had been plying to and fro across the river as required. That day the finishing touches were being put to securing permanently the cables by which they were hauled across the river.

Supervising the operation was a bearded figure whose dress seemed exotic against the browns, greys and greens of the landscape. He wore a scarlet single-breasted jacket with nine brass buttons at equal distances from collar to waist seam. The collar was two inches high, rounded in front, the edge and collar seam being furnished with round-back gold cord. The collar and cuffs were of 'garter blue velvet' and it would have been most irregular if his cuffs had exceeded $10\frac{1}{2}$ inches in circumference at the wrists. His trousers, which were tucked into brown leather riding boots, were of dark blue Oxford mixture and had a scarlet stripe, $1\frac{3}{4}$ inches

1

wide, down the outer seam. Since he was on active service he wore a brown leather shoulder belt with buckle, tip and slide in engraved gilt. His sword belt was of the same materials but he wore it under his jacket. Attached to the belt by three narrow slings was a sketching case.

On his head he wore a blue helmet with a white tropical cover. This form of headwear was an innovation, modelled, as military headwear tends to be, on that of the European army which had most recently been successful, in this case the Prussian. It might have resembled the Prussian *pickelhaube* more closely had Queen Victoria not raised objections. 'The Queen is not anxious to see the British army so much assimilated to the German and wishes particularly, in order to avoid it, to do away if possible with the spike at the top of the helmet, which Her Majesty considers neither useful nor ornamental. Perhaps some other finish to the top could be devised which would neither resemble the German helmets nor yet those of our police.' The Queen was not wholly successful in her intervention. The spike was retained but both it and the contour of the helmet itself were made less rotund than in their German forbears.

This soldierly figure was Lieutenant John Rouse Merriott Chard, Royal Engineers. He was thirty-two and in his eleventh year of service. Three of these years he had spent in Burmuda and another in Malta. The rest of his commissioned soldiering had been divided between Chatham, Aldershot and Exeter. He had only recently arrived in South Africa and there was nothing to mark him out as an officer of distinction. When he passed out of the Royal Military Academy at Woolwich in the summer of 1868 he had been eighteenth out of a batch of nineteen newly-commissioned Engineers. The only lasting impression he had made at Woolwich was that he was always late for breakfast. Lord Kitchener was remembered for the same trait but he only entered the R.M.A. as Chard left.

The course at Woolwich lasted for two and a half years and was designed to turn out competent technicians rather than leaders of men in battle. The main subjects Chard had studied were Artillery (practical and theoretical), Fortification and Bridging, Mathematics, Natural and Experimental Philosophy, Landscape Drawing, Mechanics, French and Hindustani (to which German was an alternative). Apart from a great deal of footdrill, he had attended, in addition, lectures in astronomy, mineralogy, geology and metallurgy. The Academy's course in history and geography had been abandoned six years before Chard joined but a course on Military History and the Art of War was started a few months before he left.

Lieutenant Chard was feeling rather superfluous in the early afternoon of 22 January. The securing of the cables for a ferry was scarcely a task worthy of the skills of a commissioned Royal Engineer. It could safely be left to the civilian ferryman, Mr Daniels, and to Sergeant Milne of the Buffs who was in charge of a fatigue party. Chard's task at Rorke's Drift was to build a redoubt to protect the crossing. He had spent ten days at the site and had already traced out the earthwork on the ground. It could be started as soon as men were available to do the work but there was no sign that any were likely to arrive in the near future. It was most unlikely that he would be allocated any skilled men from his own corps. Two companies of Royal Engineers had landed at Durban at the New Year and one was on the march to Rorke's Drift, but they would move on into Zululand where the vast convoy of ox-wagons was lumbering towards King Cetshwayo's distant capital along tracks which badly needed the professional attention of the sappers. The fort at the drift would have to be built with the help of British infantrymen, who were traditionally averse to working with pick and shovel, or with Basutos, who were averse to hard work of any kind.

At dawn that day a young officer, Lieutenant Horace Smith-Dorrien, had ridden in from the field column and had given the officers at the drift such news as there was. Little of note had happened but 'a big fight was expected'. He had borrowed eleven rounds of ammunition for his pistol. After he had returned, Chard decided to ride up to Isand-

3

hlwana to see his colleague, Lieutenant McDowel, who with four sappers was accompanying the column. While he was there he learned that large bodies of Zulus had been approaching the camp but that they had retired to the north and north-west. It seemed that nothing of interest was likely to happen at the camp that day. It was, however, possible that the retiring Zulus might try to work round to cut at the column's communications. It was just possible that they might attack Rorke's Drift. Chard decided to return and report the situation to his commanding officer.

Brevet-Major Spalding of the Hundred and Fourth Foot was one of Lord Chelmsford's staff officers and had been left in charge of the area Rorke's Drift—Helpmakaar as a temporary measure until reinforcements and a senior officer arrived. He was taking an early lunch at Rorke's Drift when Chard returned from Isandhlwana and told him what he had heard. Spalding thought that the single company stationed at the drift was too small a garrison for so vital a bottleneck on the field column's line of communication. Two days earlier he had sent orders to Helpmakaar for another company to come forward. They had not arrived, as the officer in charge at Helpmakaar thought that he could not spare them until reinforcements reached him. They represented half his total garrison. To resolve this *impasse* Spalding, who outranked the captain at Helpmakaar, decided to ride the ten miles back and insist on the company coming forward. It was a perfectly reasonable step to take but by taking it he deprived himself of the chance of becoming a national hero. He set off about two o'clock, instructing Chard to take command of the post.

It seemed unlikely to be an onerous charge. Spalding would only be away for four or five hours and, although he reported it, Chard does not seem to have been much impressed by the seriousness of the Zulu threat. He ordered no special precautions to be taken and busied himself with supervising the ponts, which were strictly engineering business.

He may well have felt some reluctance to assert his

4

authority as long as everything was quiet. There were two other combatant officers at Rorke's Drift and both of them had some reason to resent interference. Captain George Stephenson commanded a company of the Natal Native Contingent. The British troops thought poorly of the Contingent as a whole and Stephenson's company was known to be even worse trained than the rest of that force. Stephenson was senior in rank to Chard but he held only a colonial commission and was thus considered ineligible to command regular troops. The relative standing of regular and colonial commissions had been a bone of contention in South Africa for many years. The regulars took the uncompromising view that they were professionals and that even the youngest second lieutenant could not be put under the command of the most experienced colonial amateur. The colonial attitude was that fighting in South Africa was a very specialized business and that only they knew the country and the ways of the indigenous inhabitants. They were glad to have the support of regular troops (provided that the Government in London would pay for them) but all operations should be under colonial control. There was much to be said on both sides of this argument and tactlessness on both sides had made it a sore subject. In this case the regular view proved sound, as Captain Stephenson's subsequent behaviour showed.

Also at Rorke's Drift was Lieutenant Gonville Bromhead, commanding B Company, 2nd battalion, Twenty-Fourth (2nd Warwickshire) Foot, which formed the garrison of the post. He was at the time two years older than Chard and had eighteen months more service. Chard's seniority arose from the fact that Engineer officers were commissioned as lieutenants straight from Woolwich while Bromhead had had to serve more than four years as a second lieutenant before being gazetted to a lieutenancy in October, 1871. He was thus three years junior to Chard. While it was no longer unthinkable, as it would have been forty years earlier, for an engineer officer to command infantry or cavalry, it was still unusual. Chard and Bromhead were on friendly terms

5

and the Engineer would naturally avoid 'pulling his rank' without clear necessity, the more so since Bromhead had seen active service in South Africa and Chard had not.

Apart from the ferry across the Buffalo, Chard's responsibility that afternoon consisted of a depot of stores, under the charge of a Commissariat Officer, James Dalton, and a Casualty Clearing Station for the field column, under Surgeon-Major James Henry Reynolds. Depot and hospital were established in two buildings half a mile from the ferry. Around them were encamped the force allocated to their protection, Bromhead's company, eighty-five all ranks, and Stephenson's dubious levy, a hundred strong.

If Chard had any qualms, they can scarcely have extended to the reliability of the Twenty-Fourth Foot. Their tradition of steadiness and bravery went back through Burgos, Alexandria and Malplaquet to Blenheim. No regiment of the line could excel them for reliability. On the other hand they had been a consistently unlucky regiment. Their first operation outside the British Isles had been a disastrous raid on Brest in 1694. In 1741 they were at the mismanaged, fever-ridden siege of Cartagena in what is now Colombia, an operation which cost them twelve officers and eight hundred men. Fifteen years later they were one of the regiments which had had to surrender when Admiral Byng failed to relieve Minorca. In 1777 they had had to capitulate again with Burgoyne at Saratoga. At Talavera they lost almost half their strength in extricating the Guards Brigade from the consequences of their uncontrollable ardour. A year later, in 1810, two shiploads of their 1st battalion had been captured by a French warship off Madagascar. The colours had been thrown overboard to keep them out of the enemy's hands. None of these misfortunes were of the regiment's own making but, taken together, they suggested that if there was any bad luck to be had the Twenty-Fourth would have it.

The officers of both battalions of the regiment had dined together at Helpmakaar two days before the advance into Zululand had started. It was a few days short of the thirtieth anniversary of Chillianwallah and Captain William Degacher,

6

second-in-command of the 1st battalion, proposed the toast, 'That we may not get into such a mess, and better luck next time'. Twenty-one of the officers present were to die in action within a fortnight.

Chillianwallah, a village near the Jhelum river sixty miles south of Rawalpindi, was the scene of a desperate battle in the second Sikh war. 12,000 British and Indian troops attacked 30,000 Sikhs in a naturally strong position. The Twenty-Fourth formed part of a division commanded by Colin Campbell, later the hero of the Indian Mutiny. Having given their brigadier his objective, Campbell rode away to supervise his other brigade pausing only to tell the Twenty-Fourth to make the attack without firing a shot. They advanced through thick jungle which broke them into small detachments before they came in sight of the enemy. Refusing them time to reform their brigadier urged them on to the attack. Under a storm of grapeshot, which killed the impetuous brigadier, they advanced 850 yards, reached the Sikh guns and spiked them. They suffered heavily and had no semblance of regular order. Their flanks were in the air, as the sepoy battalions ordered to support them had not come forward. A Sikh counter-attack overwhelmed them. They had gone into action with 31 officers and 1,065 other ranks. 13 officers and 225 men were killed, 9 officers and 278 men were wounded. The Queen's Colour was lost.* Five years later one of the consolations offered to a survivor of the charge of the Light Brigade was 'It is nothing to Chillianwallah'.

The regiment had not served in the Crimea and had survived the Indian Mutiny without any major misfortune. The 1st battalion had been in South Africa since 1874 and had done good service in various small campaigns in the bush apart from suppressing a European riot in Kimberley. The 2nd battalion, to which Bromhead's company belonged, had

---

* The Colour was not captured by the Sikhs. When the ensign carrying it was killed, it was rescued by a private soldier who wrapped it round his body under his tunic for safety. He was killed soon after and, unwittingly, the colour was buried with him.

7

arrived at the Cape in March, 1878. They were short of experienced NCOs and the proportion of young soldiers in the ranks was high. They had, however, had some experience of bush fighting in the Transkei soon after they reached the continent. The whole regiment was short of senior officers and seven of the thirteen available companies were commanded by lieutenants.

Chard had been in South Africa only a few weeks and can have had no first-hand knowledge of the Zulus and their army. He must have known the general view of the British army that they represented the most formidable force which the British might have to fight. The Boers of the Transvaal were believed to live in fear of them. It was to be another three years before the British learned, at Laing's Nek and on Majuba Hill, that courage and military skill were among the Boer virtues.

The British had fought a constant skirmish with the native population ever since they had come to the Cape in 1795. Seven of their campaigns had been dignified with the name the Kaffir Wars but between them there had been almost continuous minor warfare. Seldom had formed bodies of troops been in any serious danger. There were casualties and misfortunes but never anything like a defeat for the regulars. The problems had been those of putting down a guerrilla campaign conducted in country favouring the enemy, with too few troops and a crippling shortage of cavalry and mounted infantry. Whenever any of the hostile tribes had been sufficiently unwise to mass their troops for battle in open country a British victory had followed as a matter of course. There had been no enemy, Kaffir or Boer, who could withstand British discipline and firepower. However, pitched battles had been rare and the main requisites for victory had been an efficient commissariat and an endless ability to march.

In June, 1878, Lord Chelmsford, Commander-in-Chief in South Africa, completed the putting-down of a rebellion by the Gaika and Gcaleka tribes around the Great Kei river which formed the north-eastern border of Cape Colony. The campaign had followed the traditional pattern of Kaffir wars. The rebels had taken refuge with their cattle in broken country covered with thick scrub. They had had to be surrounded, flushed from cover, separated into effective groups and harried until they lost their leaders* and became too disheartened to continue.

As soon as the fighting was over Chelmsford realized that his next task might be to subdue the Zulus. 'It is more than probable that active steps will have to be taken to check the arrogance of Cetchwayo, Chief of the Zulus.' It would, he knew, be a very different type of operation from dealing with the Gaikas and Gcalekas. The new potential enemy had a large standing army and fighting them might well include pitched battles against great numbers of trained men who had as much discipline as his own regulars. He was determined that the altered conditions of warfare should be brought home to his troops and his staff were set to preparing a document describing the Zulu army. This was printed and distributed to all officers.

This pamphlet began, 'The Zulu army, which may be estimated at from 40,000 to 50,000 men, is composed of the entire nation capable of bearing arms. At short intervals, varying from two to five years, all the young men who have during that time attained the age of 14 or 15 years are formed into a regiment which, after a year's probation, during which they are supposed to have passed from boyhood to manhood, is placed in a military kraal or headquarters. In some cases they are sent to an already existing kraal, which is the headquarters of a corps or regiment, of which they become part; in others, especially when the young regiment is numerous, they build a new military kraal. As the regiment grows old it generally has one or more regiments embodied with it, so that the young men may have the benefit of their

* The head of Sandili, chief of the Gaikas, was brought back to England as a souvenir by the commander on the spot. It now lies buried in the garden of a Cotswold farmhouse.

elders' experience and, when the latter gradually die out, may take their place and keep up the name and prestige of their military kraal. In this manner corps are formed, often many thousands strong. Under this system the Zulu army has gradually increased until at present it consists of 12 corps, and two regiments, each possessing its own military kraal. The corps necessarily contains men of all ages, some being married and wearing the head ring, others unmarried; some being old men scarcely able to walk, while others are scarcely out of their teens.

'Each of these corps or regiments has the same internal formation. They are in the first place divided equally into two wings—the right and the left—and in the second are subdivided into companies from 0 to 200 in number, according to the numerical strength of the corps or regiment to which they belong, and which is estimated at 50 each [sic], with the exception of the Nkobamokosi regiment, which averages 70 men to the company . . .

'The chief distinction is between married and unmarried men. No one in Zululand, male or female, is permitted to marry without the direct permission of the king, and when he allows a regiment to do so, which is not before the men are about 40 years of age, they have to shave the crown of the head, and to put a ring round it, and then they become one of the "white" regiments, carrying white shields, etc., in contradistinction to the "black" or unmarried regiments, who wear their hair naturally and have coloured shields.

'The total number of regiments in the Zulu army is 33, of which 18 are formed of men with rings on their heads, and 15 of unmarried men. Seven of the former are composed of men over 60 years of age . . . so that for practical purposes there are not more than 26 Zulu regiments able to take the field, numbering altogether 40,000. Of these 22,500 are between 20 and 30 years of age, 10,000 between 30 and 40, and 4,500 between 50 and 60 years of age. From this it will be seen that the mortality in Zululand is unusually rapid.

'Drill—in the ordinary acceptance of the term—is unknown among the Zulus; the few simple movements which they perform with any method, such as forming a circle, forming a line of march in order of companies, or in close order of regiments, not being deserving of the name. The officers have, however, their regulated duties and responsibilities, according to their rank, and the men lend a ready obedience to their orders.

'As might be expected, a savage army like that of Zululand neither has nor requires much commissariat or transport. The former consists of two or three days' provisions in the shape of maize or millet; and a herd of cattle, proportioned to the distance to be traversed, accompanies each regiment. The latter consists of a number of lads who follow each regiment, carrying the sleeping mats, blankets and provisions, and assisting to dress the cattle.'

The portion quoted above, amounting to more than half the whole, contains everything which could possibly have any relevance to the regimental officer except the last three, rather disjointed, paragraphs.

'A large body of troops, as a reserve, remain seated with their backs to the enemy; the commanders and staff retire to some eminence with one or two of the older regiments (as extra reserves).

'All orders are delivered by runners.

'It is to be noted that although the above were the ordinary customs of the Zulu army when at war, it is more than probable that great changes, both in movement and dress, will be made consequent on the introduction of firearms among them.'

The last paragraph, which as it happened was unjustified, threw doubt on the validity of everything which had gone before but did, for the first time, mention weapons, although not the weapons with which the Zulus were actually armed.

Lord Chelmsford's scheme for giving his army a reasonable idea of the new kind of enemy they were going to face had been admirably conceived but lamentably executed by the staff officers responsible. It is clear from the portion quoted that the information circulated would be of more interest to the sociologist than the soldier. It would be of limited interest to a company commander that Zulus tended to die young, nor would he greatly care if his assailants were married or single. The remainder of the document was of even less practical assistance. It is doubtful whether Lieutenant Chard, while checking the ponts on the Buffalo, mused at any length on the fact that the Zulu officers commanding the left and right wings of their fighting formations were known respectively as the *induna yesicamelo yesibaya 'sikulu* and the *induna yesicamelo yohlangoti*. It is possible that he derived some comfort from the information that, on the outbreak of war, all the Zulu regiments would march to Ulundi, about fifty miles as the crow flies from Rorke's Drift. 'On arrival at the king's kraal each regiment encamps on its own ground, as no two regiments can be trusted not to fight if encamped together. The following ceremonies are then performed: All the regiments are formed into an immense circle or *umkumbi*, the officers form an inner ring surrounding the chief officers and the king, together with the doctors and medicine basket. A doctored beast is then killed, it is cut into strips, powdered with medicine, and taken round to the men by the chief medicine men, the soldiers not touching it with their hands, but biting a piece of the strip held out to them. They are then dismissed with orders to assemble in the morning. The next day they all take emetics, form an *umkumbi* and are again dismissed. On the third day they form an *umkumbi* of regiments, are then sprinkled with medicine by the doctors and receive their orders, perhaps receiving an address from the king, after which they start on their expedition.' Supposing that Chard had any interest in these recondite rites, it would have been made clear to him by the information he received that morning that the whole business had been over and done with several days previously.

There was also a book entitled *The Zulu Army, Compiled from information from the most reliable sources and published by Direction of the Lieutenant General Commanding for the Information of those under his command*, which was printed in Pietermaritzburg in November, 1878. The 'most reliable sources' was a border agent, H. B. Finney and he gave a mass of information, some military, some anthropological, including a 'Who's Who in Zululand'. The circulation of this work was more limited than the pamphlet circulated to all officers. Much of the information in it would have been valuable to fighting officers had it not been so thoroughly wrapped up in useless details. It was only natural that most officers should confine their attention to the shorter work and that from its turgid style and lack of useful facts they would not, as Lord Chelmsford had intended, realize that their new enemy was a very different proposition from those they had hitherto encountered in South Africa.

There were many in Natal, and more in the Transvaal, who could have told the officers that the Zulus had evolved a highly effective tactical stereotype. The attacking force, apart from the backward-looking reserves, was divided into three bodies, the centre, known as the 'chest', and two flanking columns, known as the left and right 'horns'. The 'chest' would be held back and was preceded by a skirmishing line whose task was to locate the enemy and draw his fire. As soon as the enemy's position was known the 'horns' would encircle him, diverting his attention to all points of the compass. Then the 'chest' would move forward and crush him while his retreat, or even manoeuvre, was circumscribed by the 'horns'.

The technique of double encirclement was as old as war itself. Wellington had attempted it at Vitoria. Napoleon had almost achieved it at Ulm. The problem was that no European army could move fast enough or co-ordinate the movements of the different columns sufficiently to close the trap before the enemy took evasive action. Zulu armies were not encumbered by artillery or supply trains. The soldiers carried only their arms and their shields. They went barefoot and their uniform was little more than an abbreviated loin cloth. They could advance at a steady trot for hours at a stretch. The ground of their own country was their ally and they had an instinctive ability in the use of cover. The encirclement of a plodding column of British infantry, tied to

13

their lumbering ox-wagons, presented no problems. The Zulus might have been vulnerable to attack by lancers in large numbers but there were none in South Africa. Since encirclement was unavoidable the problem facing the British was whether their weapons, in particular the accurate but single-loading Martini rifle, were adequate to keep the Zulus sufficiently far away to prevent them using their primitive but effective weapons.

The assegai was the principal Zulu weapon. There was a light, throwing assegai, a weapon of limited utility against steady troops except as an irritant, so they relied mainly on the stabbing assegai, which had a short, thick haft and a broad, heavy blade and inflicted an evil, disabling wound. For really close work each warrior carried a knobkerrie, a heavy-headed stick which could smash a man's head open with quite a light blow.

None of these arms could match the Martini in equal fight but there was to be no question of an equal fight in Zulu-land. Against Cetshwayo's 40,000 effectives, Chelmsford's entire disposable force consisted of 5,400 regular infantry and gunners and 1,200 colonial cavalry. To this he could add almost 10,000 native levies who were poorly armed and under-trained. Many of them went in open fear of the enemy, although a few, recent refugees from Cetshwayo's oppression, could be expected to give a good account of themselves. The success of the campaign depended on the ability of the regular infantry to keep the enemy at a distance and to inflict on them a higher proportion of casualties than they could accept. If this could not be done the battle would be a matter of stabbing assegais against outnumbered bayonets. In such a *mêlée* there could be no doubt of the result. Only concentrated fire-power could win the war for the British.

None of this was clear from the staff's pamphlet on the Zulu army. Most of Chelmsford's men had met the assegai and the knobkerrie in earlier campaigns and had not been much impressed with them. Even in thick bush, where ambushes are easily laid, stabbing weapons are at a disadvantage against rifles. Used *en masse* by what amounted

14

to a large regular army under rigid discipline which was able to manoeuvre with unprecedented mobility and to accept casualties with equanimity and even fervour, these weapons took on a new degree of menace. Few of Chelmsford's men doubted the Zulu's bravery and determination. The speed of their movement and the bloodchilling efficiency of their apparently primitive weapons took everyone by surprise.

Chard was not giving much attention to problems of fire-power as he stood beside the Buffalo soon after three o'clock on the afternoon of 22 January, 1879. It was a hot afternoon and he had trouble keeping his attention turned towards the dreary business of securing the cables. If he thought of the Zulus at all he would have been considering how best to secure the ponts safely if an impi came that way. Suddenly he heard the beat of hooves on the hard ground. Two sweating, exhausted horses were making their best pace on the far bank, approaching from his right. The riders, both in khaki slouch hats, shouted across the river and turned their mounts to splash across the drift. At first Chard could not grasp their message but eventually they came within speaking distance. One of them he recognized as Lieutenant Aden-dorf of the Natal Native Contingent. He gasped out the news that the camp at Isandhlwana had been overrun and that a huge column of Zulus, which his companion, Sergeant Vane, estimated at 4,000 warriors, was moving fast towards Rorke's Drift.

CHAPTER 2

An Army in Transition

The army of which Chard, Bromhead and B Company, 2nd battalion Twenty-Fourth Foot formed a small part was a force in the middle of a long and ineffective period of reform. Twenty-five years earlier it had failed in the Crimea. Twenty years later it was to fail in South Africa. Both these wars were to end in technical victory but in each case the machinery of military administration collapsed and defeat was only averted by the steadfastness and discipline of the regimental officers and their men. At Sebastopol even this eventually failed when the slender supply of trained soldiers was exhausted and the final assault was a British defeat redeemed only by a French victory.

The army which failed in the Crimea had been essentially the same army which had triumphed forty years earlier at Waterloo. Parliament and people had got used to the idea that their army was invincible and, in an age when retrenchment was the watchword, saw no reason for spending money on what had already shown itself to be incomparable. To those who claimed that its control structure was archaic and chaotic it could be pointed out that the Duke of Wellington had made it work brilliantly so that it was clearly sound at bottom. If Wellington ever did a disservice to the army it was because his genius could co-ordinate the multifarious strands of administration and impose on them a unity which lesser men could not hope to achieve. He created the illusion that the impossible was possible for men who were merely highly talented.

16

In the years between Waterloo and his death in 1852 Wellington did what he could to keep the army as an effective force. He re-armed it with a rifle as good as any in Europe. He increased its mobility by ensuring that, at last, the boots issued to it distinguished between the left and right feet. He did something for the comfort of the soldier by giving him a bed to himself instead of the wooden crib holding four men which had been his resting place for decades. He made a start at educating the officers. Until 1850 the only educational qualifications for a potential officer (and even this was not specifically stated) was the ability to read and write.* The Duke insisted that ensigns and lieutenants should be examined in 'Euclid, algebra, logarithms, mensuration, trigonometry, geography and history'.

At every turn he was thwarted by those who insisted that the Army Estimates should be reduced while deploying the troops all over the world. While he held political power he introduced a pension for long service. Hitherto soldiers had only been eligible for pensions if they were disabled through no fault of their own. Wellington forced through a pension of one shilling a day after twenty-one years service with good conduct. It was too much. Grey's reforming ministry cut the pension to sixpence. Wellington came to believe that 'the greatest enemies the army has in this country are those who would add unnecessarily to its expense.' He realized that any scheme to reform the army would defeat its own ends but he warned the politicians that their cheeseparing would unfit the army when it was most needed. In almost his last speech he roundly told the House of Lords that 'We have never, up to this moment, maintained a proper peace establishment. That is the real truth. I tell you that for the last ten years you have never had in your army more men than enough to relieve the sentries on duty in your stations in different parts of the world.'

Wellington, in his capacity as Commander-in-Chief, could

* The small proportion of officers who entered Sandhurst had to be 'well-grounded in the knowledge of grammar and common arithmetic [and] to write a good legible hand.'

17

only hope to control the infantry and cavalry. None of the supporting arms or services formed part of his command. The artillery and engineers were controlled by a different member of the government. The reserve army came under the Home Secretary, supply and transport were a Treasury responsibility. The control of the medical services was so obscure that it was difficult to say where responsibility lay. Although Wellington could influence the artillery and engineers since successive Masters General of the Ordnance were his former subordinates, he could do nothing with the other services and it was these which crippled the army in the Crimea.

The blame lay with the Treasury. There lay total responsibility for supplying the troops with food and firewood (so that they could cook their food), for providing forage for the thousands of horses essential to a nineteenth century army and for transporting all provisions and stores except the ammunition actually in the limbers of the artillery or the pouches of the infantryman. To perform this enormous task they maintained, for reasons of economy, only the most vestigial peacetime establishment. At the outbreak of war everything had to be improvised. When the great naval convoy carrying the expeditionary force reached Malta, notices were posted in the streets of Valetta and the other towns which read 'Parties desirous of joining the Commissariat Department, under the orders of Commissary General Filder, about to proceed with the force to the east, as temporary clerks, assistant storekeepers and interpreters may apply freely to Assistant Commissary Strickland.' It was not to be expected that such recruiting among the unemployed of Malta would lead to a high standard of competence in the supply services.

Once this ragamuffin staff had been hired, Treasury practice made their task impossible. The doctrine on which the Commissariat worked had proved reasonably sound in Marlborough's wars but had failed in every major overseas campaign which had been undertaken subsequently. It was that both food and transport could be obtained on arrival in the theatre of war. The army landed in the Crimea with no more transport than the limbers of the artillery, the forage wagons of the cavalry and the light carts on which infantry battalions carried their immediate reserve of ammunition. It came as an ugly surprise to Commissary General Filder that no Russian contractor came forward with an offer of sufficient wagons to move the supplies for an army of six divisions. Even before the Crimean winter came it was almost impossible to bring rations and ammunition forward to the troops. When the gales and snows set in even the wounded could not be moved without help from the French. The army starved, sickened and died but the officials of the Treasury could console themselves by computing the amount the taxpayer had been saved by not maintaining a peace-time organization for supply and transport.

What the Treasury had started, the medical services consummated. The regimental surgeons were, almost without exception, conscientious, skilled and hard-working. Above them was a hierarchy as complicated as that of the army itself. One of its heads was the Inspector General of Hospitals, a man with forty years service, none of it as a regimental surgeon. He had no high opinions of the recent advances in medical science and circularized his subordinates that 'Dr Hall takes this opportunity of cautioning medical officers against the use of chloroform in the severe shock of gunshot wounds, as he thinks few will survive where it is used. However barbarous it may appear, the smart of the knife is a powerful stimulant, and it is better to hear a man bawl lustily than to see him sink silently into his grave.'

The doctors, however, were responsible only for the treatment of patients. More men sank silently to their graves through the failures in hospital administration than from the combined efforts of the smart of the knife, the chloroform bottle and the enemy. The non-medical running of the hospitals was divided between the Commissary General, who had more than enough to do in other directions, and another Treasury official, the Purveyor General. The person selected in Whitehall for this post in the Crimea was a septuagenarian. He was provided with a staff of two clerks and three messengers and surrounded by a code of minute regulations designed for a peacetime setting in England.

In 1856 the Secretary of State for War announced the cost of the Crimean campaign in terms of manpower. 'From 19 September, 1854, the day on which the army was first engaged in action, to 28 September, 1855, there were 158 officers and 1,775 men killed; died of their wounds, 51 officers and 1,548 men; died of cholera, 35 officers and 4,244 men; died of other diseases up to 31 December 1855, 20 officers and 11,425 men; died of their wounds up to 31 March 1856, 322 men: making a total loss of 270 officers and 19,314 men. . . . . In the same time there were discharged from the service as incapacitated from disease and wounds 2,873 men.'

This proportion of more than four men who died from disease to every one who died from enemy action was not unusual in British military history. In the Walcheren expedition of 1809 there had been 106 battle deaths and 3,950 from disease. The difference lay in the information which reached the public in Britain. The existence of an electric telegraph from Constantinople meant that the news of the battle of the Alma reached London in the same time that it took the public to learn of the battle of Waterloo. The news of the army's sufferings outside Sebastopol raised a storm of public fury which brought down Lord Aberdeen's government and put in its place that of the ageing Lord Palmerston who, with most of his colleagues, had been members of the Aberdeen ministry. Palmerston was only able to survive in office by adopting his predecessors' technique of blaming all the shortcomings of the supply and medical services on the generals in the Crimea.

That they were able to use the generals as a scapegoat was largely the triumph of *The Times* correspondent, William Howard Russell. He had great journalistic talent but he had no discretion and was wholly unscrupulous. Moreover he had a grudge against the headquarters of the army and, in particular, against the Quartermaster General, Richard

1. Lt John Rouse Merriott Chard

2. Lt Gonville Bromhead

Airey.* Russell accused him, publicly and privately, of every kind of incompetence and inattention. Palmerston's government saw him as a convenient scapegoat. The new Secretary for War, Lord Panmure wrote to Lord Raglan 'my strong advice [is] that you should try to get a more energetic and efficient officer than Airey seems to be.' Raglan refused to part with his Quartermaster-General who was unquestionably the most efficient staff officer in any of the armies in the Crimea, but the witch-hunt against him continued and only faded when a Court of Enquiry showed the ludicrous flimsiness of the evidence against him.

When Raglan defended Airey, Russell turned his attack against the Commander of the Forces. Lord Raglan, he wrote, 'does not go among the troops. He does not visit the camps, he does not cheer them. [He has] not been down to Balaklava, has never visited a hospital ... I am sure of my facts.' Each one of these statements was a lie and it is scarcely possible that Russell did not know it, even though he spent almost the whole of his own time in the meagre comforts of Balaklava consorting with malingering officers whom he encouraged to write disloyal letters to his newspaper. The government took Russell's 'facts' as established truth. Lord Panmure accused Raglan of neglecting his troops. 'It would appear that your visits to the camp were few and far between, and your staff seem to know as little as yourself of the conditions of your gallant men.' To a man as gentle and considerate as Lord Raglan nothing could have been more wounding and his army resented such treatment in a way he was too generous to be able to do.

The relevance of the Crimean *débâcle* to the Zulu war and to every other British campaign of the second half of the nineteenth century lies in the sense of betrayal felt in the army, especially in the higher ranks, at the Palmerston

* Before setting out for the Crimea Russell had obtained from the War Office a promise that rations would be provided for him. This promise was not communicated to Airey who refused to supply them until ordered to do so from London. He was subsequently censured for supplying them by the (civilian) Auditor General.

government's search for scapegoats. For decades an over-stretched army had been starved of money and subjected to a control structure that made even the simplest operation a bureaucratic obstacle race. When a major operation had to be undertaken, even if it was one like the Crimea which both naval and military commanders believed to be unsound in conception, the glaring inadequacies of the system were exposed and the generals were publicly pilloried for the shortcomings of departments over which they had no control.

The tragedy was that the public outcry over the Crimean war gave an opportunity for reforming the army at a time when funds might have been available to do the job properly. As a result of the hostility between the politicians and the soldiers the opportunity was lost. Reforms were effected but they were partial and ineffective. The artillery and engineers were put under the Commander in Chief and Commissariat officers became responsible to the War Office in the first instance although their activities were still circumscribed by minute Treasury regulations. A Land Transport Corps, for which Lord Raglan had pleaded before sailing for the Crimea, was belatedly established. A government small-arms factory, which he had proposed before the war began, was set up at Enfield and the business of clothing soldiers was taken away from the colonels of regiments and given to an Army Clothing Board with its own factory at Pimlico. A large tract of land at Aldershot, which the army had asked to acquire in 1853, was bought as a training area and, for the first time, the army had land on which it was possible to exercise a whole brigade at the same time. Some small improvements were made to barracks after it had been pointed out in the House of Lords that the space allotted to soldiers was 400 square feet each while convicts were allowed 1,000 square feet. The ancient office of Secretary at War was amalgamated with that of Secretary of State for War. No explanation was offered of how Lord Palmerston had managed to hold the Secretaryship at War for nineteen years without noticing that it was redundant.

The moment for effective reform passed and political and

financial considerations resumed their old paramountcy over military matters. In 1856 the Duke of Cambridge, cousin to the Queen, was appointed Commander-in-Chief. He proposed that the troops at home should be divided permanently into Brigades and divisions, each with a staff attached to them. The Secretary of State replied that 'although this would be the more regular course of procedure, it would give a handle for the ignorant to pull at, and it will be more prudent to avoid it.' The army had to continue without experienced staff officers.

The most stringent and mindless economy was enforced. As Chancellor of the Exchequer, Mr Gladstone complained bitterly that he had 'never heard a reason intelligible to me for maintaining in time of peace the present number of subalterns'. There were only two to each company of infantry. He kept an eagle eye on the minutest detail of military spending. On one occasion he came across a proposal from an engineer officer who submitted that, since the wooden bridge across the moat at Fort Augustus frequently rotted and had to be rebuilt, it should be replaced by a stone bridge. Gladstone was outraged. In his own hand he wrote to the War Office denouncing it as 'a case of wanton extravagance on the part of the officer who recommended it, who, I submit, ought to be called upon for his reasons and, if they are not satisfactory, reprimanded.'

Despite all the political and financial obstructions, the army's efficiency was steadily increasing. In 1860 Sir Hope Grant, a general who combined an almost total lack of education with conspicuous talent as a cellist, conducted a tidy little campaign in China in which the medical and supply services worked with notable efficiency. Eight years later Sir Robert Napier performed one of the most remarkable military feats of the century. 15,000 fighting men, starting from an improvized port on the Red Sea, advanced to the Abyssinian capital of Magdala, building themselves a road as they went. They took with them, apart from mountain guns, a battery of nine-pounder breech-loaders, two 8 inch mortars and a naval rocket battery. Although the military opposition was not very severe, it was an administrative triumph. The force included Indian troops, both Muslim and Hindu, whose dietary requirements greatly complicated the supply problem but at no time did the rations fail. As Napier wrote in his General Order to the troops when the campaign was over, 'You have traversed under a tropical sun and amidst storms of sleet and rain, 400 miles of mountainous, rugged country. You have crossed ridges of mountains, many steep and precipitous, more than 10,000 feet in altitude. . . . Not a single complaint has been made against a soldier of fields injured or villagers wilfully molested either in person or property.'

The Ethiopian compaign was one which no other European army could have undertaken successfully. The other side of the coin was that the military power of Britain was rightly regarded as negligible on the continent. In 1864 Prussia and Austria were threatening to seize the duchies of Schleswig and Holstein from Denmark. Britain, whose Prince of Wales had recently married a Danish princess, was gravely affronted. Palmerston, still Prime Minister at the age of 79, declared that 'it would not be Denmark alone with whom they had to contend'. The German powers ignored the threat. They were planning to move against the Danes with 200,000 men. Britain, they knew, could not field more than 20,000 and those only after a substantial delay.

It was this insult to Britain's pretensions which decided the Liberals to reform the army when next they came to power. They were re-elected in 1868 on a slogan of 'Retrenchment and Reform' and, while both these principles applied to the army, they also determined to have a force capable of intervening in continental wars. To carry through this remarkable programme they appointed as Secretary for War, Edward Cardwell, a lawyer with no military experience but with a clear sharp brain, absolute integrity and a determination to do his best for the army and the country. That he failed to carry out all three tenets of the declared policy can not be attributed to his fault.

He was hampered by the reluctance of the senior officers

24

to co-operate with a man who had been the colleague of Palmerston and, although the Duke of Cambridge gave him loyal if unenthusiastic support, he was forced to rely for his military advice on Sir Garnet Wolseley. Wolseley was the perfect soldier for politicians. A field commander of ability he succeeded in convincing himself and the newspapers that he was a Great Captain. His greatest talent was for public relations but he was malicious, overbearing, conceited and intemperate in speech. Wolseley, wrote Disraeli to the Queen, 'is an egotist and a braggart. So was Nelson.' The fallacy was the supposition that because Wolseley had Nelson's vices he also had his virtues. Unfortunately this was not the case. Where Nelson welded men together in service, Wolseley split them apart.

Many, perhaps most, of his ideas for reform were sound and he pursued them ruthlessly. Conciliation was foreign to him. Those who disagreed with him were, by his definition, fools or worse. Publicly he treated them with barely concealed contempt. Behind the scenes he lost no opportunity of denigrating and mocking them. Since he took the view that all those who were not wholeheartedly with him were against him, he alienated many senior officers of moderate and even progressive views who were far from being the empty-headed reactionaries he painted them.

At the same time he built up round himself a clique of young officers who basked in his reflected glory. They were almost all highly competent staff officers and Wolseley lost no opportunity of pushing them into influential vacancies in and out of season. To be a member of the Wolseley ring, to be a devoted admirer, was a sufficient qualification. In the Ashanti campaign Redvers Buller, whose bone-headedness was surpassed only by his courage, was made head of the Intelligence Department. Wolseley's favourite among the 'ring' was George Pomeroy Colley whom he described as 'the ablest man I know'. It was not until 1881 that Colley was given a chance to show his full abilities. He was killed on Majuba Hill leading the most inept manoeuvre in British military history since Whitelock tried to storm Buenos Aires in 1807.

Wolseley, with all his virtues, did the army a serious disservice. He divided it into two hostile camps. For the last quarter of the nineteenth century no commander who was not a fully accredited member of the Wolseley circle could undertake a campaign without the knowledge that Sir Garnet was using every endeavour to poison the minds of his political chiefs against him and his staff in the hope that they could be supplanted by members of the ring.

The most successful of Cardwell's reforms was administrative. The War Office and the Commander-in-Chief's department (the Horse Guards) were integrated. This resulted in the War Office writing 30,000 fewer letters and minutes in a single year. None of his other actions had such spectacular results. He abolished the system whereby a soldier enlisted for what amounted to life, substituting a twelve year term of which six would be spent with the colours and the remainder on the reserve, ready to be called out in times of emergencies. In theory this was an admirable arrangement but it overlooked the situation of the army. India and the colonies required such a high proportion of the army's strength that only long service would provide the garrisons and most men preferred to sign on again for full time service rather than risk the uncertainties of civilian life after the dubious joys of barrack life in India. This tendency was accentuated by the reluctance of employers to give any but the most menial work to men who might at any time be called back to the army. While the change did have the effect of ridding the army of a number of undesirable 'old sweats', it also squeezed out of the regiments too high a proportion of experienced sergeants and corporals and filled the ranks with young soldiers. Even Wolseley reported from South Africa in 1877 that 'I have just made a careful and minute inspection of the half battalion of the 13th Light Infantry stationed here. I inspected the recruits by themselves, of whom, I am sorry to say, there is a greater proportion than is good for any corps. Most of them I consider to be at present unfit for the hard work of the campaign, although I see no reason why they should not be very efficient soldiers in another year or eighteen months, when they have finished growing and their muscular powers have been improved by good living.' The introduction of short service did increase recruiting to some extent although there were many who suggested that the increase had been caused, not by short service, but by reducing the height standard from five foot, eight inches to five foot, four. In any case, Cardwell failed in his main aim—to create a reserve. When the Boer war broke out in 1899, almost thirty years after the scheme was introduced, only 80,000 reservists were available, a number insufficient to replace the number of regulars who, from their youth and low physical standard, could not be used in the field.

In his endeavour to create a force in Britain which would be available for use on the continent, Cardwell laid down that battalions should be linked in pairs* and that one battalion of each pair was always at home. To achieve this, garrisons were withdrawn from the more developed colonies such as Australia, Canada and New Zealand, the Royal Navy was handed the task of protecting many of its own coaling stations and the garrisons of several colonies, notably South Africa, were cut to, and beyond, the bone. It was a tidy scheme and looked well on paper but it was doomed to failure since it overlooked the huge and ever-changing demands of the colonial empire. The balance of battalions was never struck and by 1879 there were eighty-two line battalions overseas and fifty-nine in the British Isles, only six more than had been at home before Cardwell's scheme was launched. It was plain in South Africa how badly the plan was working since in 1879 both battalions of the Twenty-Fourth were stationed there.

The reform which attracted the widest attention was Cardwell's decision to abolish the system whereby commissions and promotions were bought and sold. Its abolition had

* The paired battalions were not formed into integrated regiments until after the Zulu war but the senior twenty-five regiments of the line already had two battalions so that no linking was necessary.

27

for decades been the sacred cow of the radical left but its opponents had been vocal for centuries. William III, Queen Anne and George I had all tried to do away with it. By the middle of the nineteenth century it was an obvious anachronism and survived only for the reason which had called it into being, the parsimony of Parliament. To abolish it required a substantial sum of money to recompense those who had invested in commissions and a further recurrent sum to provide pensions for officers of long service who were no longer required. In fact, purchase officers, who did not form as high a proportion of the officer strength as is commonly supposed, had served the army and the nation well over the centuries, and the shortcomings of the army stemmed at least as much from elderly non-purchase officers who could not afford to retire since pensions were given only for disablement.

Whatever its value as a political gesture, the abolition of purchase made very little difference to the type of officer who led the army. If the forty-four officers of the infantry and cavalry* who died during the Zulu war are taken as a representative sample, it will be seen that 24 received their first commission before abolition and twenty† subsequently. It would be very difficult to distinguish between the social background of these two groups of officers. The fathers of both groups were more likely to be country gentlemen than to have any other occupation, although in both, army officers and clergymen made up a substantial category. In each group the father of one officer was a peer, of two were baronets and of one a member of Parliament. Five of the dead officers in each group had been educated at Eton. Ten in the pre-abolition group and eight in the other had attended other well-known public schools. The rest were educated either privately or at small schools which specialized in getting

* These were the only two arms of the service in which purchase had existed. It was never possible in the artillery and engineers and had been abolished for regimental surgeons and chaplains at the end of the nineteenth century.

† There were also two quartermasters commissioned from the ranks but such promotions had been common for more than a century.

young gentlemen into the army.* There was rather more higher education among the pre-abolition group, Oxford, Cambridge and Edinburgh each having a representative, while of the later twenty there was one who had been to Cambridge and one who had attended the Royal Agricultural College. In each category only seven had been to Sandhurst. Most of the rest had had a few months training in the militia. Of the twenty-four who became officers before abolition only five had purchased their first commission.

Although the quality of the officers was unchanged, field commanders had reason to be troubled about their forces and their prospects in the years that followed the Cardwell reforms. The Crimea had shown that generals could not count on government backing if things went wrong. The activities of Wolseley and his 'ring' meant that the worst complexion would be put on any misfortune, however caused, and what Sir Frederick Roberts referred to as the high proportion of 'boys in the ranks' must have made commanders wonder whether their men would have the same stamina and steadfastness as those who had faced out so many disastrous situations in the past. It was not a happy time to be a general.

* One of the pre-abolition group had been educated for the Royal Navy in HMS *Britannia*.

29

CHAPTER 3

The Colonies Britain Did Not Want

A historian once remarked that Britain acquired her empire in a fit of absent-mindedness. She acquired South Africa in spite of her best endeavours. The fact was that nobody wanted the Cape of Good Hope. Even the aboriginal inhabitants showed no great enthusiasm for the immediate environs of what is now Cape Town. The Cape was only important or desirable as a staging post on the spice route to the Indies but until the middle of the seventeenth century no European power valued it highly enough to make a settlement there. It provided water but little else. The Portuguese used it occasionally but they considered the harbour treacherous and, after a lethal skirmish in 1510, the inhabitants hostile. St Helena provided better staging facilities until the trade grew so heavy that the island could no longer supply sufficient foodstuffs for the passing ships.

After the crew of the wrecked Indiaman *Haarlem* found that the natives were friendly and the soil fertile the Dutch East India Company set up a trading post at the Cape in 1660. In addition to a pier, some warehouses and a small fortress, the settlement included some market gardens and arable land so that it could be self-supporting and supply the passing trade. All the inhabitants were Company employees and the agriculture was conducted for the Company's benefit. It did not thrive but the Dutch policy was to keep the station isolated from its hinterland and trading with the natives was prohibited. Such 'nationalized' farming became so obviously unprofitable that the Company was induced to persuade farmers to emigrate from the Netherlands in exchange for freehold farms but on condition that all their produce was sold to the Company at the Company's prices.

From that time warfare became endemic in South Africa. The imported farmers were not satisfied for long with their controlled market. Illegal trade with the natives started and thrived despite anything the authorities could do to prevent it. Worse still, the farmers realized that the land was highly suitable for the raising of cattle. This meant that increasing amounts of land were needed for grazing and the more land that was used, the more were the contacts with the natives.

Moreover, raising cattle meant giving hostages to fortune. There is little that human predators can do to arable farming or market gardening except destroy the crops, an unprofitable proceeding for all concerned. Cattle, on the other hand, can be stolen with reasonable facility and become an asset to the thief. Cattle stealing had been a major industry in the area for centuries and the tribes saw no moral difference between stealing Dutch cattle and stealing the herds of their neighbours. For a time the fact that the settlers had muskets and horses went some way to deter the cattle thieves but they soon managed to acquire both advantages for themselves.

The Dutch authorities maintained their policy of keeping their trading post isolated and refused to give protection to the expanding farmers since they were acting illegally. At the same time they continued to assert their right to tax the farmers who consequently took steps to avoid taxation by moving further from the seat of government and took their own steps to protect themselves and their cattle.

The British came on the scene first in 1795 when they seized the Cape from the Dutch who were then the allies of revolutionary France. Only a tiny force was needed, for the Governor, who had an empty treasury, willingly surrendered in exchange for a promise to underwrite the paper currency. The British inherited the problem of the outlying farmers and were glad to pass the Cape back to the Dutch at the Peace of Amiens. As one of the generals wrote, 'It is hardly

31

possible to convey an idea of the ignorance, the credulity, and the stupid pride of these people, and particularly of the Boers. The most absurd ideas of their strength and importance are prevalent among them, nor indeed is there any opinion on any subject too ridiculous or too grossly unjust not to be adopted by them.' The renewal of the war with France forced Britain to take the Cape again in view of its importance as a post on the route to India. This time they kept it. In 1814 the Dutch ceded the colony in perpetuity in exchange for £2,000,000 which they undertook to spend on their defences on their frontier with France.

For a time relations between the British and the Boers went reasonably smoothly despite the British insistence on collecting taxes, which increased the Boer reluctance to live under any form of government. They also found incomprehensible the British doctrine of the equality of all races before the law, a doctrine the British themselves seemed to practise only by fits and starts. In particular they regarded the trial and punishment of Boers for maltreating or murdering Africans as an infringement of natural liberty. There was an ugly incident in 1815 when a party of African soldiers was sent to arrest a farmer called Bezuidenhout who had repeatedly refused to answer a summons issued by a British magistrate. Bezuidenhout fired on the soldiers who returned the fire and killed him. His relations raised a rebellion on the specific grounds that it was unchristian to arrest a white man with blacks. The rising was put down with ease, the British having much Boer assistance since the rebels had, illogically, called a Basuto chief to their help. There was, nevertheless, a wave of Boer indignation when five of the rebels were executed with remarkable incompetence at Slagter's Nek.

The crunch came when Britain abolished slavery in 1833. The Boers did not greatly object to emancipating their slaves as it was not difficult to evade the intended consequences. But although they kept their slaves as 'servants' or 'apprentices' under very much the same conditions as before, they resented bitterly that the compensation payable was

32

only a third of the assessed value of the slaves. To increase the bitterness, the compensation could only be collected in London, thus necessitating the employment of agents who required large commissions on the amount they collected. In 1834 there began a mass migration of Boers, the Great Trek, to the north. It was a brave attempt to move off into the unknown to escape the interference of government.

No attempt was made to stop the Trekkers. Opinion at the Cape was almost unanimous that the colony was well rid of them and could now develop as a cohesive entity. This, however, was not the view of the British Parliament. The government took little interest in the Cape except for its naval value but their well-meaning supporters insisted that something should be done to prevent the Boers from maltreating the natives. Thus in 1837 there was passed the Cape of Good Hope Punishment Act which made all British subjects liable to the laws of Cape Colony anywhere in Africa south of the 25th parallel of latitude. Since they had set out from Cape Colony the Trekkers counted as British subjects, however hard they tried to reject that particular blessing.

There has seldom been a piece of legislation passed with such lofty motives and so unrelated to reality. The 25th parallel crosses Africa somewhat north of where Pretoria now stands and four hundred miles north of the nearest British post. It laid on the Governor of the Cape the duty of protecting the natives of a vast area, far beyond his reach, against people who blandly refused to recognize his authority. The force available to him consisted of three understrength battalions and the Cape Mounted Rifles who were already fully occupied within the colony. From London he was constantly pressed to agree to a reduction of the size of the garrison.

It was all that the Governor could do to keep the peace along his existing frontier. Since it was his duty to stop the settlers molesting the natives, the settlers naturally looked to him to protect them from the natives who continued their traditional cattle raiding. There were not enough troops to

33

mount a cordon along the frontier and all that could be done was to mediate where possible and mount the occasional punitive expedition. Frontiers could be agreed with native chiefs but the treaties were seldom observed for long on either side and inexorably the frontier inched forward irrespective of the wishes of the Governor or the London government.

The tribes of South Africa were almost all nomadic, moving with their herds from pasture to pasture. To nomadic peoples a frontier is a difficult concept to grasp and this applied as much to the Boers as to the Basutos. British officials made continual and determined efforts to negotiate frontier lines but it was like doing business with a cloud. Even if an agreement could be reached to stop cattle-raiding across a given line, it did not follow that the chief with whom the agreement was made would still be in power, or even that the same tribe would be anywhere near the line a few years later.

Meanwhile the authorities at Cape Town were under pressures which made it impossible to pursue any coherent policy. Successive administrations urged the Governor to reduce his commitments, to confine his activities to protecting the naval base with a minimum of troops. The colonists, while creeping slowly northward, demanded protection from the natives. The religious lobby in Britain, which grew more influential as the nineteenth century progressed, insisted that the frontiers of the colony should be pushed northward to control the Boers. As a result governor after governor found himself committed against his will and in excess of his resources to a forward policy which must, in the end, lead to major troubles with the Boers if with no one else.

As it happened a new type of African power was developing to the north at just the time that the Boers were turning their thoughts in that direction. Fifteen years before the Great Trek started, a young man called Shaka came to the head of the Zulus, a tribe of fine physical specimens but of little consequence and comfortably remote from the white settlements. At that time they belonged to the Mtethwa

Confederation, a group of tribes which had been welded together into a coherent unity under a remarkable personality, Dingiswayo. Dingiswayo not only imposed his rule over a wide area, he backed his power with a standing army. Within his own territory he maintained a peace and stability unknown in South Africa and made determined but unsuccessful efforts to build up trade with the Portuguese at Delagoa Bay. On his frontiers he fought and won great and bloody battles against neighbouring tribes but in victory he adhered to the convention of native wars. Women and children were spared and he seldom deposed rival chiefs if they would agree to become his vassals. He seized vast numbers of cattle but the fruits of victory he valued most were the young men of the defeated tribes who were conscripted to swell his army.

Soon after Dingiswayo's death, Shaka succeeded to the headship of the Mtethwa Confederation which he named kwaZulu, Zululand. At this time he controlled all the land between the Tugela and the Pongola rivers, which latter flows into the sea at Delagoa Bay. He also controlled Dingiswayo's great army which he expanded and improved. The stabbing assegai was issued for the first time and the warriors were forbidden to wear sandals. Shaka struck north and south, devastating the territory of neighbouring tribes and seizing their cattle. Unlike Dingiswayo he waged total war. Villages were razed to the ground. Men, women and children were butchered. A horde of refugees surged to the south spreading stories, some of them exaggerated, of the cruelty of the Zulus. It was the beginning of a legend, largely based on fact, which was in the end to make it seem essential to break the Zulu power.

In 1828 Shaka's impis struck as far south as the Umzimkulu river, which later became the southern boundary of the colony of Natal. So alarming were the reports of their raid that a British force was sent against them, only to find that they had already retired.

If Shaka massacred his neighbours he was scarcely more merciful to his own people. He imposed a reign of terror. If a man was thought to be contemplating thwarting the king he was executed. Shaka's cruelty and suspicion grew with the years. The death penalty was introduced for sneezing while the king dined. Four hundred women were executed at one time on suspicion of witchcraft.

The climax came when Shaka's mother died. Shaka proclaimed public and prolonged mourning. Those who did not weep and continue to weep were clubbed to death. One of the king's counsellors was forced to kill seven of his wives and all their children because their grief was insufficiently apparent. Since tears were not enough, the king decreed that the entire nation would forswear agriculture, milk drinking and sexual intercourse for a year. Indulgence in any of these activities was liable to the death penalty. Shaka was murdered by his aunt and two of his half-brothers.

Whatever Shaka's eccentricities in domestic policy, he was careful to keep on good terms with the few Europeans who came in contact with him. His armies were cautioned against involving themselves with white men.

Dingane, one of his assassins, took Shaka's place but lacked his half-brother's prudence. He started his reign by proclaiming an era of peace and internally this was achieved after he had executed all those who could conceivably dispute his claim to the throne. Since he could not afford to keep his army idle, his foreign policy was aggressive.

By this time a small European trading post had been established at Port Natal, on the present site of Durban. Some trade was done with the Zulus although it was frequently interrupted when Dingane tried to enforce his own interpretation on agreements reached with the traders. In 1831 he lost his temper with the white men. He had sent for one of them and claimed that instead of attending the royal summons the trader had gone hunting. Immediately he sent two regiments to destroy Port Natal. Warned in time, the white community took to the bush with their coloured servants and there were no human casualties. The Europeans of Port Natal, with the support of the Governor of the Cape, petitioned London to be made a Crown Colony. The government, seeing only another isolated territory which would have to be defended, refused the petition.

Six years later a much more serious incident occurred. The Great Trek was in full flood and the Voortrekkers came over the Drakensberg into Natal. A delegation led by Piet Retief visited Dingane seeking permission to buy land. The king refused to discuss the matter until the Boers had recovered for him some cattle stolen by a neighbouring chief. This they did. In February, 1837, Retief, with seventy-one Boers, thirty coloured servants and the stolen cattle returned to the king's kraal. Dingane, thereupon, signed a document making over to them all the land south and west of the Tugela, roughly the subsequent area of Natal. Having done this Dingane invited the visitors to witness a war-dance. Half way through the dance the entire party, Boer and coloured, was murdered in the sight of a missionary family who were not molested.

Immediately Dingane sent his army against the Boers in Natal hoping to wipe them out. In this he was disappointed. Only forty-five men, fifty-six women and a hundred and eighty-five children with two or three hundred coloured were massacred. 35,000 cattle and sheep were seized. In April of the same year an impi raced down to Port Natal, looted it and destroyed the buildings. Most of the settlers took refuge in a trading vessel which happened to be off-shore.

The murder of Reteif and his companions permanently poisoned the atmosphere between the Zulus and both white races. Up to that time British, Boers and Zulus had expected to find some kind of *modus vivendi*. There had been occasional clashes and misunderstandings as was to be expected in dealings between three races whose ways of thought were almost incomprehensible to each other, but trading in skins and ivory could be to the advantage of all and there was plenty of room for all three.

Horror stories from Zululand had been circulating in South Africa since Shaka's time. In future no tale of treachery and bloodshed was too lurid to be believed. Until

37

1837 the Zulus had been regarded as savages but the term 'savages' was not in the early nineteenth century perjorative. The concept of the Noble Savage was only sixty years old and the Zulus with their magnificent physique and rigid discipline had some pretensions to nobility. To massacre unarmed men while they were enjoying one's hospitality transgressed the rules of even the most primitive societies. After 1837 the Zulus were no longer savages, they were barbarians, utterly untrustworthy.

Naturally the Boers retaliated and, for a time, the British at Port Natal co-operated with them. The immediate operations failed but in December, 1838, a great battle was fought on the Ncome river which, with good reason, was subsequently known as Blood River. A Boer commando of 500 men with 53 wagons under Andries Pretorius fought off and utterly defeated 10,000 Zulus. Dingane thereupon made over Natal to the Boers and promised to send a large indemnity in cattle, a promise he did not keep. To keep his army occupied, he sent it against the Swazis, who defeated it and eventually killed Dingane himself. He was succeeded by yet another half brother, Mpande, who had been considered so feeble-minded as not to be worth liquidating. He accepted the throne as a vassal of the Boers and gave Zululand thirty years of comparative peace.

The second raid on Port Natal persuaded the government in London to send a single company of regulars to the town. The company commander, Captain Henry Jervis, was instructed to mediate between the Boers and the Zulus. Negotiating from a position of great weakness, Jervis failed and the troops were withdrawn. The Boers therefore declared Natal to be an independent republic, set up an administrative capital at Pietermaritzburg and asked Britain for recognition.

Both at the Cape and in London the British authorities favoured recognizing the new state. They saw no point in incurring expense to secure Durban (as Port Natal was beginning to be called) which had a poor harbour. It seemed probable that the Zulu power was in eclipse rather than extinguished and that sooner or later Natal would need a substantial garrison for no obvious gain. Legally the Boers could be considered as British subjects but there was no reason to assert this fact. They had proved themselves difficult subjects to rule and notably incompetent in the business of civil administration. The sensible course seemed to be to leave them to stew in their own juice.

London was two years in making up its mind about recognition and during this time the embryo republic had succeeded in arousing the liberal and non-conformist consciences of Britain. First they made a punitive raid south into the uncolonized land between the south of Natal and the north of Cape Colony. They seized 3,000 head of cattle and killed thirty men. They also abducted seventeen children whom they apprenticed to farmers. Many in Britain were unable to distinguish between apprenticeship and slavery. At the same time the republic was becoming concerned at the size of its native population. In 1841 the *Volksraad* passed a resolution that all 'surplus' Africans should be sent to live in the south of the republic. They should be moved by persuasion if possible but force could be used if necessary.

It was more than tactless of the *Volksraad* to take this step before recognition had been granted. Evangelicals and non-conformists alike arose in their wrath and insisted that the Boers were British subjects and that the Cape of Good Hope Punishment Act was still in force. The government bowed before this righteous storm.

On 4 May, 1842, three companies of the Inniskillens occupied Durban from the sea. Pretorius attacked them but, despite heavy casualties, they managed to stand a siege until reinforcements arrived a month later. In May, 1843, Natal was proclaimed a British colony. The majority of the Boers, who had already travelled vast distances to escape just that status, trekked back over the Drakensberg. The British were left with a common frontier with Zululand and, although the new colony flourished, few of its inhabitants, white or coloured, did not at times fear that one day the impis might again come pouring over the Tugela.

39

For a short time British governments showed some interests in the east coast of South Africa. In the middle of the century the coming of steam meant that the Royal Navy lost the unchallenged supremacy at sea which it had enjoyed since Trafalgar. It became a major strategic consideration that harbours in the Indian Ocean did not fall into the hands of other powers. Although the British did not trouble to improve the port of Durban until the end of the century, they felt happier that they owned it. They even negotiated to buy Delagoa Bay but could not see their way to paying the price the Portuguese asked.

Meanwhile complications for Britain were building up elsewhere. When the Voortrekkers had moved into Natal they left behind them a ramshackle community north of the Orange river. The inhabitants of 'Transorangia' lived in a legal vacuum. The majority of the inhabitants did not explicitly reject British sovereignty and the Cape authorities did nothing to assert it except when the Boers interfered too blatantly with their coloured neighbours.

In 1848 a new Governor of the Cape paid a visit to Transorangia, armed by London with wide discretion. He was Sir Harry Smith, one of the most attractive characters in British military history. *Chevalier sans peur et sans reproche*, he had a distinguished military record in the Peninsula, in America, in India and in South Africa. He was, however, no politician. He was given an enthusiastic welcome in Bloemfontein. In some part this was due to a minority who genuinely wished to remain under British rule. Much more was a personal welcome to himself for he had many Boer friends and admirers who remembered his outstanding leadership of a joint Anglo-Boer force in 1835. He misread the friendship shown to himself personally as enthusiasm for British rule and decided to assert British control over the area under the name Orange River Sovereignty.

The annexation would probably have been accepted by the vast majority of the inhabitants, albeit with a poor grace. Unfortunately Smith had hardly returned to the Cape when Andries Pretorius and the Voortrekkers returned over the

Drakensberg, escaping from the new British colony of Natal. Furious at finding that his previous base had also become British, Pretorius raised a rebellion and swept the British garrison, sixty men of the Cape Mounted Rifles, out of Bloemfontein.

Smith reacted with speed and efficiency. He collected 800 regulars and marched against Pretorius. He came up with him at Boomplatz on 29 August, 1848, and routed him with contemptuous ease. British rule over the Orange River Sovereignty was re-established. It lasted for six years, until the government in London realized that to protect the settlers from African cattle raiders a permanent garrison of 2,000 men would be needed. This was too much for the British taxpayer to stomach. Sovereignty was relinquished and the territory became independent as the Orange Free State.

Boomplatz had two undesirable effects. The British formed a low opinion of Boer fighting ability, an opinion which was reinforced in 1858 when a force from the Orange Free State disintegrated when invading Lesotho. The evidence of the battle of Blood River was disregarded. Since the British were no more prepared to see the Zulus destroy the Boers than see the Boers destroy the Zulus, it remained at the back of British thinking that they might one day have to use troops to rescue the Boers from the formidable barbarians to the north.

The other consequence was that the irreconcilable Boers moved off to the north, across the Vaal river. In the hope of escaping from British interference they established the South African Republic, better known as the Transvaal. It was a curious state, its constitution being largely based on a mistrust of all forms of government. The only factor making for cohesion was the detestation all its inhabitants felt for British rule. For twenty years the British did not attempt to interfere with the Transvaal despite the fact that the republic's constitution stated specifically that 'The people are not prepared to allow any equality of the non-white with the white inhabitants.'

The foreign policy of the Transvaal in its early years con-

41

sisted of a spirited attempt to annex the Orange Free State. This was unsuccessful but meanwhile the new republic was pushing forward its boundaries. In particular they acquired a common frontier with Zululand along the Blood and Pongola rivers. In time Boer settlers crept over across this riverline into the Zululand. They claimed that they had treaty rights to this infringement and certainly Mpande was too weak to resist them.

If only the British could have cast off all thoughts of being responsible for the Boers, nothing could have assured the safety of Natal more surely than the arrival of the Boers on the northwest borders of Zululand. Bad feeling was the least that could be predicted for Transvaal–Zulu relations. Although Zulu relations with the white races in the past had been marked by capriciousness, their instinct for self preservation must dictate that they would do their best to avoid the hostility of both white races who were known to be on distant terms with each other. The British record in their dealings with the native races was far from perfect but it was very much better than that of the Boers, and the non-conformist lobby could be trusted to see that it stayed that way. It might even be tempted into using British strength to resist Boer encroachments into Zululand. While there were pressures for an expansionist approach from the British settlers at the Cape and in Natal, the official government policy, resting on the twin pillars of Economy and a High Moral Tone would insist on maintaining the *status quo* for as long as possible and, perhaps, for rather longer.

CHAPTER 4

The Black Empire and the White

Ten years before the outbreak of the Zulu war, the whole situation in South Africa changed. Up to that time its importance to Britain or to any other European power was as a staging post on the route to India and the Far East. Successive British governments troubled themselves as little as possible about the colonies there apart from ensuring the safety of the harbours. They wanted to have nothing to do with the hinterland which seemed to be good for very little except subsistence farming and ivory trading. Urged on by the nonconformist lobby they hoped to stumble on some way to protect the natives from the settlers. They also accepted a reluctant duty to protect the settlers from the natives.

In 1869 their interest slumped when the Suez canal was opened and the Cape route to India became of secondary importance. It became of even less consequence in 1875 when Disraeli acquired control of the Canal. Henceforward the strategic importance of South Africa was limited to its potential nuisance value in the hands of an enemy who might use it as a base for raiding in the Indian and Atlantic Oceans. In 1878 heavy guns were installed at Cape Town as a defence against the Russian fleet.

Simultaneously the mineral wealth of South Africa came to light. A diamond was found at Hopetown in 1866 and four years later Kimberley became the centre of a diamond rush. In the following year Griqualand West, which included Kimberley, was annexed by Britain to the fury of the Boers of the Orange Free State whose frontier lay within sight of the diamond fields. In 1873 gold mining was started at Lydenburg in the Transvaal. British and foreign speculators descended on the republic which was in no condition to absorb them.

In the sixties the Transvaal was little more than a geographical expression. Although it had a skeletal administrative organization, it was little more than a loosely knit community of farmers bound together only by the requirements of defence. The incursion of miners threatened to wreck the whole way of life. The farmers had never produced more than was vital for their own needs. Even had there been a farm surplus, links with the outside world were so tenuous that it would have been impossible to export it. The settlement of miners, traders and their hangers-on brought economic chaos.

Prices soared. In less than ten years a township of 18,000 people sprang up at Kimberley. Eggs cost a pound a dozen and cabbages could be sold for seven shillings. Kimberley, moreover, was British and could count on British help to avoid ruin. No such outside help was available for the Transvaal. The President, the Rev. Thomas Francois Burgers, was devoid of administrative and financial skills. He came to the conclusion that the country could only be saved by building a railway link with the outside world at the Portuguese port of Lourenço Marques on Delagoa Bay. To achieve this he went to Europe and, in Holland, raised a loan at disadvantageous terms secured on 3,000,000 acres of state land. He immediately spent much of the loan on the purchase of rolling stock and used the rest to pay the exorbitant interest. Returning to Pretoria he found that the baPedi tribe under their chief Sekukini had erupted on to the pledged state lands and were settling themselves across the track of the proposed railway. To eject them, Burgers called out the commandos, the traditional Boer substitute for an army. The Boers were unenthusiastic about the campaign. They wanted the railway as little as they wanted the gold miners. There was no threat to their own farmsteads, only state lands were involved. The fighting was left to mercenaries and some hired Swazis who deserted when the mercenaries stole their cattle to compensate themselves for the pay which Burgers could not produce. The campaign was a fiasco and completed the bankruptcy of the Transvaal.

The British were still groping their way towards a way of cutting down their expenses in South Africa. Apart from the potential naval bases their disinterest was almost complete. In spite of the discovery of the mineral fields a *Times* correspondent could still write in the late seventies that the South African colonies 'are never likely to compete with America or Australia in the emigration market. They have to contend with every difficulty to which a country can be subject. There are harbours with sand bars which it is improbable that any outlay will remove. There are rivers without water, plains without grass, hills without trees or shelter. There are, as in the Karoo, hundreds of miles of sand separating one end of our jurisdiction from another, and defying all hopes of improvement.'

Nevertheless, Britain could not wash her hands of her colonies. Her settlers demanded protection and an even noisier lobby of humane, liberal-minded men demanded that the natives should be protected against the settlers, both British and Boer. The Cape of Good Hope Punishment Act had never been repealed and this gave a basis for the humanitarians to insist that the British government should interfere with those Boer customs, such as a thinly disguised slavery, which seemed sinful to earnest gentlemen in London.

The only way out seemed to be to follow the Canadian example. It was only recently that the two hostile communities in Canada had accepted federation and undertaken to be responsible for their own defence in return for virtual independence. It was Lord Kimberley, Colonial Secretary in Gladstone's first government, who first conceived the idea of applying the same solution to South Africa but Gladstone lost power in 1874.

Disraeli, the next Prime Minister, as befitted the man who had bought the Suez Canal, was profoundly disinterested in South Africa. He left its problems to his Colonial Secretary,

45

Lord Carnarvon, whom he always referred to as 'Twitters'. Carnarvon eagerly embraced the idea of uniting Cape Colony, Natal, the Orange Free State and the Transvaal into a Federation of South Africa which would have almost complete independence under the Crown. He sent the historian James Anthony Froude out to report on the prospects. Despite optimistic early reports, Froude achieved nothing. The two republics did not wish to join and Cape Colony, which already had a large measure of self-government, ignored the proposal in a very pointed manner. The Prime Minister was displeased. His private secretary wrote, 'Lord B* is extremely dissatisfied with all that has taken, or is taking, place at the Cape. The trouble commenced by Lord Carnarvon, who, he says, lived mainly in a coterie of editors of liberal papers who praised him and drank his claret, sending Mr Froude—a desultory and theoretical *literateur* who wrote more rot on the reign of Elizabeth than Gibbon required for all *Decline and Fall*—to reform the Cape, which ended in a Kaffir war.'

Unrestrained and undeterred, Carnarvon abandoned Froude and put his trust in Theophilus Shepstone who had made his reputation as Secretary for Native Affairs in Natal, a post in which he had earned the trust of the Zulus. Carnarvon instructed him to arrange federation and gave him secret authority to annex the Transvaal provided that the population appeared to support the idea.

In January, 1877, Shepstone, who spoke fluent Afrikaans, reached Pretoria and found the government at a standstill. The *Volksraad* refused to accept any of President Burgers' measures and put forward none of its own. There was 12/6d in the treasury. The wages of the civil servants were months in arrears and all the prisoners had been released from the jail as they could not be fed. He did his best to assess public opinion but it was an impossible task. As he wrote at the time. 'The white strength consists at the outside of 8,000 men capable of bearing arms. Of these about 1,000 live in towns and villages, and 350 are the foreign and fluctuating

* Disraeli was created Lord Beaconsfield in 1876.

46

population collected at the gold fields. The remaining 500 are farmers widely scattered in isolated homesteads over a surface equal to that of Great Britain and Ireland put together.'

Feeling in the gold fields was unanimous for annexation. In Pretoria, where the population consisted largely of unpaid civil servants and shopkeepers on the verge of ruin, self interest dictated a friendly welcome for Shepstone. The bulk of the population, the scattered farmers, were implacably opposed to any sacrifice of independence but they could not make their voice heard. Shepstone took the feeling of Pretoria and Lydenburg as representative of the whole country and resolved to proclaim annexation. President Burgers was co-operative. Shepstone reported that he 'came to me to arrange how the matter should be done. I read him the draft of my proclamation and he proposed the alteration of two words only, to which I agreed. He told me he could not help issuing a protest to keep the noisier portion of the people quiet, and you will see the grounds for this precaution when I tell you that there are only half a dozen native constables to represent the power of the state in Pretoria. [He] read me the draft of his protest, and asked me if I saw any objection to it, or thought it too strong. I did not dissuade him.'

There was never a chance of winning Boer agreement to annexation. For a time the Boers accepted it with sullen resignation. Shepstone had acted for what he saw as the best. He saw his move as an attempt to help and protect the Boers but he had neither the skill at administration to revive their shattered finances nor the charm to conciliate the irreconcilables. Britain acquired a few thousand unwilling colonists, a heavy call on her taxpayers to re-establish the Transvaal economy and the dubious privilege of using British troops to disposess Sekukini and the baPedis of the state lands. The Prime Minister was not pleased. 'If anything annoys me more than another, it is our Cape affairs, where every day brings forward another blunder of Twitters. The man he swore by was Sir T. Shepstone, whom he looked upon as heaven-born for the object in view. We sent him out entirely for Twitters' sake, and now he has managed to quarrel with the English, Dutch and Zulus; and now he is obliged to be recalled, but not before he has brought on, I fear, a new war. Froude was bad enough, and has cost us a million; this will be worse.'

The annexation of the Transvaal knocked away the prop on which the peace of that part of Africa rested. Previously the Zulus had been on the worst of terms with the Transvaal Boers with whom they had a long-standing territorial dispute. On both sides feelings were inflamed by memories of Retief's murder and the battle of the Blood River. There was a substantial body of opinion in Zululand which favoured sending their army into the Transvaal to destroy the Boers once and for all. They had been restrained by fears of a British counterstroke from Natal and by the advice of Theophilus Shepstone.

In the new situation they saw themselves being surrounded by British power but, far worse, they felt themselves betrayed by Shepstone. He had been their friend, adviser and advocate for more than twenty years and they had implicit faith in him. In particular he had pressed their claim to the strip of ground on the east bank of the Blood river which had been settled by the Boers. The Transvaal government had claimed that the land had been ceded to them by the Swazis before the Zulus had driven them away. The Swazis subsequently asserted that they had made no such cession and the Zulus claimed the strip as their territory. Only Shepstone's advice had stopped the Zulus from regaining the ground by force. He had urged them to rely on diplomacy and British mediation to restore their rights. So great was their love for him that when they heard of his mission to Pretoria the Zulu army was massed on the Transvaal frontier and its services offered to their friend should he have trouble with the Boers. He declined their help and asked them to withdraw their troops. They complied, but it was the last time Shepstone was able to influence the Zulus.

As soon as he was installed as Administrator of the Transvaal, Shepstone embraced the Boer claim to the Blood River strip with all the enthusiasm with which he had previously supported the Zulu claim. His motives for this reversal were confused but it is unlikely that they were dishonourable or merely opportunist. He was an honest man even if he was sometimes very unwise. Partly he may have been anxious to placate Transvaal opinion by supporting their claim which had some appearance of legality on the evidence then available. Partly it may have been because his viewpoint had been radically changed by circumstances. For forty years, since he had been appointed Kaffir interpreter in Cape Town at the age of eighteen, he had been involved in native affairs. Suddenly his responsibilities had widened. He was responsible, and by his own act, for a population 'widely scattered in isolated homesteads over a surface equal to that of Great Britain and Ireland put together'. In the Transvaal he caught for the first time the terror of the Zulu army which was so widespread there and in Natal. A Zulu raid across the Blood river could cause appalling devastation. Nor had he the means of resisting it. The Boer military system had been shown in the worst possible light in the campaign against Sekukini and appeared useless. The British strength at his command consisted of eleven understrength companies divided between Pretoria, Lydenburg, Middleburg, Standerton and Utrecht. If the Zulus invaded there was certain to be a bloody massacre and he, Shepstone, would be held responsible by every Boer and by the Government in London. However creditable his motives, his adoption of the Boer case marked him irrevocably as a traitor to the Zulus.

To make the situation worse, the Zulus were once more a power to be reckoned with. The feeble Mpande was dead and since 1872 the throne had been held by his son, Cetshwayo, who had shown himself to be a formidable warrior. In British South Africa he was believed to be a bloodthirsty monster in the mould of Shaka and Dingane. His bloodthirstiness had been demonstrated in the early years of his

49

reign but it is probable that he had also inherited a strong strain of irresolution from his father, Mpande. He commanded the largest standing army in Africa and that army was restless. The Zulu system whereby young warriors were not permitted to marry until they had 'washed their spears' in human blood put the king under mounting pressure to launch his 40,000 fighting men in one direction and another. It was not unnatural that those who lived around Zululand should fear that the attack would come in their direction and be anxious that steps should be taken to remove the constant menace. If Cetshwayo did not want war, there was a strong possibility that his army might force him into one. To men living in fear the case for a pre-emptive strike grew with the years.

The man in whose hands rested the decision as to whether the Zulus should be suppressed before a possible tragedy occurred was Sir Bartle Frere. Carnarvon had appointed him Governor of the Cape in 1877 and had given him the additional title of High Commissioner for South Africa. Frere was a member of a family distinguished for its administrative and academic abilities. He had completed a distinguished career in India by being successively Commissioner for Sind and Governor of Bombay. He had all the determination and uprightness which characterized the Indian civil servant, but his service in the sub-continent had heightened the intellectual arrogance which characterized his family.*

One sentence in Frere's commission as High Commissioner was particularly relevant to the situation in Natal and the Transvaal. Carnarvon had charged him with 'preventing the recurrence of any irruption into Her Majesty's possessions of the [South African] tribes . . . and for promoting as far as possible the good order, civilization and moral and religious instruction of the tribes, and, with that view, for placing them under some form of settled government.' It is quite certain that Carnarvon, and far less, Lord Beaconsfield,

* Notably in his uncle, Hookham Frere, who had been Minister to the Spanish Junta in 1808 and greatly contributed to the difficulties of Sir John Moore in the Coruña campaign by his advice and admonitions.

did not regard this as a licence to annex Zululand so that it could be put under British 'settled government' but the wording in no way prohibited such a step.

Frere, on the basis of almost all the advice he received in South Africa, formed the view that it was impossible to implement this part of his commission as long as the Zulus maintained a huge army. The Boers were unanimous in fearing an invasion. The people of Natal were coming to the same conclusion. As long as the Transvaal had been independent it could be argued that Cetshwayo needed a large force to defend himself against a Boer invasion. When the Transvaal was annexed and the Zulu army remained at full strength, fear began to build up in Natal. It was strongest among the isolated farmers near the border but it was not long since Dingane had shown that not even Durban was safe from the impis.

There were two minority groups who were for taking no steps against the Zulu power. One, which was led by the Lieutenant Governor, Sir Harry Bulwer, believed that the Zulus were a threat but that any precautions for defence against them would be a provocation. The other group consisted of the immediate circle around the man who, according to some ecclesiastical authorities, was Bishop of Natal.

Few men knew more about the Zulus than John William Colenso and no one was more consistent in proclaiming his view that they meant no harm. Unfortunately his position was so anomalous and his views so idealistic that it was difficult to give full weight to his opinions. As a modern biographer has said, 'He pursued the rational (or what appeared to him to be rational) without regard to the reasonable.'*

He had been a brilliant mathematician at Cambridge and had made a name for himself by writing a mathematical textbook which continued in school use for years after his death. In 1853 he was translated from an obscure vicarage in Norfolk to the new bishopric of Natal, an appointment

* Peter Hinchcliffe D.D., *John William Colenso*, Nelson, 1964.

for which there was very little competition. During his first three months in Pietermaritzburg he published a Zulu–English dictionary with 10,000 entries and translated St Matthew's gospel into Zulu. Within seven years he had completed the translation of the New Testament and made a start on the Old. In addition, he had published a Zulu liturgy, several Zulu grammars and textbooks in Zulu Astronomy, Geography, Geology and History.

Simultaneously he had produced in English a commentary on the Epistle to the Romans and a critical examination of the Pentateuch and the Book of Joshua. The views he expressed in these works resulted in his being tried in Cape Town for heresy, although contributory factors had been the 'No Popery' riots which resulted from his conduct of services in Durban and his publicly expressed view that polygamy was no bar to conversion to Christianity. The court of bishops found him guilty and deprived him of his bishopric but the Privy Council set aside the verdict on technical grounds. The Church of England, however, refused to accept the Privy Council's intervention and appointed the dean of Pietermaritzburg as vicar general of the diocese. When Colenso went to his cathedral he found the doors locked against him. It took legal action to gain him admittance and more to secure him the use of the organ and bells. A compromise was eventually reached whereby the dean (or vicar general) and the bishop (or heretic) held services at different times. Even so there were unseemly incidents. When the dean arranged for a visiting bishop to hold a confirmation service, Colenso's churchwardens decided that it would be a good time to wash the cathedral floor. The ceremony was conducted in several inches of water. It was hard for Frere to take the views of so eccentric a character in so anomalous a position at their face value.

Frere, in any case, had made up his mind. Of those who doubted the Zulu danger he wrote that their attitude could only be accounted for by 'the sort of toleration a man extends to his pet wolf. "He is like a dog in the house," and only eats his neighbours' sheep and occasionally the cottagers'

4. Surgeon-Major J. H. Reynolds who was in charge of the hospital and who attended imperturbably to the wounded during the assault

3. (below) Lt-General Lord Chelmsford, KCB, the Commander-in-Chief in South Africa

5. The Natal Native Contingent in 1879

6. An engraving of the area around Rorke's Drift drawn by Major North Crealock of the 95th Regiment shortly after the conflict

children.'

Meanwhile Cetshwayo was doing nothing to convince his neighbours of his peaceful intentions. His reputation as a man of blood had been established before his accession. In 1856 he had established his position as heir apparent at the battle of Ndondakuaka fought against his half brother. The whole of the defeated army, with their families, had been pinned against the unfordable, crocodile-infested Tugela and massacred by his troops. Reliable estimates of the dead ranged between 20,000 and 25,000 the majority of them being women, children and old men. Six of his half brothers had been among them.

Until the annexation of the Transvaal he had admitted some kind of British suzerainty over Zululand. In particular he had invited Shepstone to perform his enthronement, as representative of the British Queen. Before doing so, Shepstone had addressed the Zulu state council and obtained their enthusiastic consent to new laws aimed at introducing a more humane form of justice. Indiscriminate bloodshed was to cease, minor crimes were no longer to carry the death penalty* and even for serious crimes no man was to be executed without the previous knowledge and consent of the Zulu king. These new laws were proclaimed to the people at the enthronement ceremony and Cetshwayo accepted them at least by implication.

There was no appreciable diminution of quasi-judicial killings in Zululand and it was clear that Cetshwayo did not admit the validity of the new laws. More in sorrow than in anger, Sir Henry Bulwer remonstrated with him about a particularly brutal batch of killings and got a highly intemperate reply. 'I do kill, but do not consider that I have done anything in the way of killing yet. Why do the white people start at nothing? I have yet to kill; it is the custom of our nation and I shall not depart from it. . . . My people will not

* The wife of Bishop Colenso regarded this kind of thing as unjustified interference. She wrote, 'Cetshwayo, of course, has no prisons nor other material for dealing with criminals and those who break the 6th (or 7th) commandment have to be knocked on the head.'

53

listen unless they are killed; and while wishing to be friends with the English I do not agree to giving my people over to be governed by laws sent by them. Have I not asked the English to allow me to wash my spears since the death of my Mpande, and they have kept playing with me all this time, treating me like a child? I shall now act on my own account. . . . The Governor and I are in like positions: he is Governor of Natal and I am Governor here.'

This was an open threat to use the Zulu army but Bulwer, true to his policy of appeasement, replied by offering to set up a boundary commission to adjudicate the dispute over the Blood River strip. For the inhabitants of Natal, Cetshwayo's letter confirmed their worst fears. Frere agreed with them and while confirming Bulwer's offer of a boundary commission came privately to the conclusion that the Zulu army would have to be disbanded or destroyed in the near future. He was encouraged, unintentionally, in this decision by a letter from the Colonial Office which told him that 'It is only too probable that a savage chief such as Cetshwayo, supported by a powerful army already excited by the recent successes of a neighbouring tribe* over the late government of the Transvaal, may now become fired with the idea of victory over H.M. Forces, and that a deliberate attack upon H.M. territory may ensue.' Having drafted this despatch Lord Carnarvon resigned the Colonial Office and Sir Michael Hicks Beach was appointed in his place.

Frere had served in India throughout the great Mutiny of the Bengal army. His friends had been slaughtered at Meerut, Delhi and Cawnpore. He was not prepared to be responsible for the massacre which would occur if the Zulu army plunged across the long and indefensible frontiers with Natal and the Transvaal. 'My mistrust is not because they are semi-savages, but because they are a military nation and Cetshwayo's whole object is to keep up their military character. They generally believe themselves to be invincible— under similar circumstances I would not trust to any people, to any King or Emperor in Christendom, to abstain from

* Sekukini and the baPede.

54

aggression. I do not believe that anything will induce them to abstain unless they are thoroughly convinced of our superior power: and I do not see any chance of their being so convinced till they have tried their strength against us and learned by sad experience.'

It is easy to assert with hindsight that Cetshwayo had no intention of invading British territory and that the army would continue to suffer his restraint indefinitely. Such assertions cannot be proved. Sir Bartle had a terrible decision to take. Zulu intentions were unknowable. The information he had, largely gathered from missionaries, suggested that the Zulu temper was bellicose. This was confirmed by the tone of Cetshwayo's intemperate letter. If he decided to wait on Zulu moves and invasion came, a massacre of black and white was unavoidable. There were not enough troops to stop it at or near the frontier.

Cetshwayo obligingly provided him with a series of incidents which could be used as an excuse for forcing a show-down. The most significant was when two runaway Zulu wives fled across the Tugela in July, 1878. Armed Zulus crossed after them, dragged them back and executed them under the eyes of border guards who were too few to intervene.

When Cetshwayo refused to make adequate reparation or to hand over the culprits, Frere sent an ultimatum which was delivered to Zulu representatives, together with the report of the boundary commission, on 11 December, 1878. The report was an unsatisfactory document. It affirmed that the Blood River strip was Zulu territory but claimed that the intrusive Boers were within their rights to live there. Bulwer had intended the commission as an emollient. Its report was an irritant.

The ultimatum set out the minimum conditions that Frere believed could make the British colonies safe from attack. The Zulu army was to be demobilized and, to obviate the necessity of 'washing the spears', 'every man, when he comes to man's estate, be free to marry'. It also demanded that the new laws, proclaimed at Cetshwayo's enthronement, should be reaffirmed and enforced. An answer was required within twenty days.

Frere hoped that Cetshwayo would agree to these demands. Neither he nor his Commander-in-Chief wanted immediate war. Two battalions and two companies of desperately needed Royal Engineers were at sea and could not reach the borders of Zululand until at least forty days after the delivery of the ultimatum. Nor were the demands unreasonable. Even Bishop Colenso said that 'I hoped and believed that Cetshwayo would agree to these demands, and expressed my cordial assent to the main points of the message —namely those requiring the disbandment of the military forces and an entire change in the marriage system as being, though measures of coercion, yet such as a great Christian power had the right to enforce upon a savage nation like the Zulus.'*

No satisfactory reply having been received after twenty days, a further period of ten days was granted for a reply. There was still no sign of agreement and on 11 January responsibility for securing compliance passed to the Lieutenant-General Commanding in South Africa.

---

* This report of Colenso's opinion was recorded by Frere, who might not be considered a reliable witness. On the other hand it was quoted in the House of Commons by the Colonial Secretary and was denied neither by the Bishop nor by Mrs Colenso who conducted a long campaign to show that the Bishop disapproved of all Frere's actions.

CHAPTER 5

Pre-Emptive Strike

At the head of the troops in South Africa was Sir Frederic Augustus Thesiger, 2nd Baron Chelmsford,* a major-general of eleven years standing with the local rank of lieutenant-general. He was a soldier of proven courage and administrative ability and came from a family with a long and distinguished record of service. His paternal great-uncle had served with Rodney in the American war, in the service of Catherine the Great against the Swedes and on Nelson's staff. At the battle of Copenhagen his knowledge of Baltic navigation had been invaluable to Nelson and at the height of the battle he was entrusted with the Admiral's message to the Danish Crown Prince, proposing a truce. This message he had delivered in a pinnace under the terrible fire of the Trekroner battery. After the battle he was made post-captain and knighted.

This Captain Sir Frederic Thesiger took his nephew, later the 1st Lord Chelmsford, into his ship as a midshipman but after some years the young man left the navy and was called to the bar. Nevertheless he married into a military family. One of his wife's uncles, after the initial setback of being captured at Saratoga, rose to be a lieutenant-general having seen active service in the West Indies, at the Helder, on Walcheren and in the Peninsula. His son was killed leading the Eighty-Third Foot at Vitoria. Another uncle died gallantly as a major repelling the French invasion of Jersey

* He succeeded his father in the title on 5 October, 1878. For convenience he will be referred to as Lord Chelmsford throughout this narrative.

after his colonel had surrendered the island.

The general was not the only one of the former midshipman's sons who joined the army. Another commanded the Sixth Dragoons and their sister married Colonel Inglis who led the defence of Lucknow after the death of Henry Lawrence. A third brother followed his father into the law and became a Lord Justice of Appeal. In this he did not achieve the same legal heights as his father who was twice Lord Chancellor, although, as one of his obituaries remarked, he was 'an important politician though never a statesman'. More importantly, he earned the dislike of his political chief, Disraeli, who carried forward his enmity to his eldest son, the General.

General Lord Chelmsford was commissioned into the Rifle Brigade in 1844 at the age of seventeen. He soon transferred to the Grenadier Guards with whom he continued until 1858 when he exchanged into the Ninety-Fifth (Derbyshire) Regiment as a lieutenant-colonel. He had bought his regimental commissions but he was given a brevet majority after his service in the Crimea, a fact which shows that he had merit as well as wealth. In the Indian Mutiny he commanded the Derbies in the confused fighting in central India and stayed on in the sub-continent, mostly in staff posts, marrying the daughter of a major-general in the Bombay Army. In 1868 he was selected for the staff of the expedition against Abyssinia.

As has been mentioned, the campaign to Magdala was a very notable administrative feat and, as Deputy Adjutant General, Chelmsford must be able to claim a considerable share of this organizational triumph. Sir Robert Napier, a commander who was not lavish with praise, referred in his despatch to Chelmsford's 'great ability and untiring energy'. It earned him the senior and taxing post of Adjutant General, India, and ante-dated promotion to major-general.

He was appointed to the command at the Cape after four years commanding troops in England. On arrival he found the ninth Kaffir War in progress in Cape Colony and it was not until he had brought this to a successful conclusion that he could turn his attention to the situation in the north. When he was able to go to Pietermaritzburg at the beginning of August he found the border dangerously unguarded. Beyond the Tugela lay the Zulu army with a field strength of 40,000 men and there was a general anticipation in Natal that they might invade at any moment. If they came there was nothing to stop them. The capital was wide open to them. Even Durban could scarcely be considered as safe. As he wrote, 'At P.M.burg there were four companies of the Buffs, at Newcastle four companies of the 80th regiment; at Utrecht three companies 90th Light Infantry. The 1/13th were in the Transvaal at Pretoria, Middleburg and Lydenburg.' In all there were less than 2,000 men without a single squadron of cavalry. Five times the number of infantry could not have guaranteed the security of the frontier.

The problem of defence against a Zulu invasion, wrote Chelmsford, 'is a very complex one and may be said to be practically unsolvable.... It is necessary to bear in mind that the border line between Zululand and the colonies of Natal and the Transvaal is upwards of 200 miles long in a straight line, and about 300 miles by road, and that the country close to the Natal border is so broken as to render lateral communication, except by one road* which runs at some distance from Zululand, almost impracticable.... The Natal frontier cannot be watched by a force placed in a central position, such as Greytown, ready to be moved to any part of the line which might be entered or invaded, as the country and roads do not admit of such an arrangement. All that can be done in the way of passive defence is to watch and defend, as far as possible, the three main points of entry, viz.—the Durban road; the Fort Buckingham–Greytown–P.M.burg road; and the Umsinga or Sands Spruit valley.

'A native force, however, entering Natal from Zululand, could always avoid these points; and could with perfect ease

---

* 'A narrow wagon track from the Lower Tugela Drift, via Greytown to Helpmakaar, a distance of about 158 miles, keeping on an average about ten miles from the river, but out of sight of it the whole distance.'

and without the smallest risk, make a serious raid into the Colony and get back across the river without the smallest chance of being molested by the defending forces. In 1838 the Zulus under Dingane successfully invaded Natal at two different points, viz.—the Sand Spruit valley and by Lower Tugela Drift. The first body reached as far as the present town of Estcourt, the second reached Durban. A glance at the map will show that every part of this 200 miles frontier is about equidistant from Ulundi [the Zulu capital and the army's concentration point] and that consequently Cetshwayo, being on interior lines and quite independent of roads or wagon tracks, could direct his whole force on any part of the line, which might seem to offer him the best results.'

As he summarized the situation later, the problems of defence were insoluble. 'In the month of August, when I assumed command, the distribution and number of the Imperial and Colonial troops gave no hope of my being able to prevent an invasion should Cetshwayo give orders for it to be made.'

It is impossible to fault Chelmsford's reasoning on the military situation. The troops available could no more hold back the Zulus than the piers of Westminster Bridge could hold back the Thames. His opinion must have carried more weight with Frere than the pious hopes of the new Colonial Secretary. Hicks Beach, disturbed by the legacy Carnarvon had left him, wrote to express 'a confident hope that, by the exercise of prudence and by meeting the Zulus in a spirit of reasonable compromise, it would be possible to avert the very serious consequences of a war with them.' Viewed from Pietermaritzburg, prudence and reasonable compromise seemed a poor defence against the stabbing assegai.

Having decided that if there was to be a war, the British would have to attack, the next question was one of timing. While it was important that the troops on their way to South Africa, especially the Engineers, should have time to reach the frontier and get acclimatized, it was equally important that the campaign should not be left too late. The fuel on which the army's transport depended was grass. If the start

60

was postponed beyond late April 'the grass on which the wagon oxen and the horses of the mounted men would depend is dry enough to burn, and would be burned by the Zulus and the difficulties of moving the troops would thus be a hundredfold increased.' There was also much to be said for launching the invasion before the Zulus had got their harvest in, that is to say before March.

Chelmsford knew that he could not conduct an offensive campaign with regulars alone. The garrison of Natal and the Transvaal consisted of less than five battalions of infantry,* two batteries of 7 pounders and one of rockets. There were no mounted troops and he asked for a regiment of Indian horse. 'A native cavalry regiment with their sharp swords would be invaluable in Zululand as the country is open, and the Zulus certain to give cavalry an opportunity of showing what it can do.' He was, however, forced to admit that 'there will be great difficulty in keeping the mounted branches effective. I understand that there are only four months in the year in which horse sickness does not prevail—June, July, August and September being free from it.' The home government refused to send any cavalry. It was only with the greatest reluctance that they allowed the two battalions of infantry and two companies of Engineers to embark for the Cape in December.

The numbers would have to be made up with colonial volunteers and native levies. Here Chelmsford needed the active help of the Lieutenant-Governor of Natal and, true to his belief that defensive preparations would provoke Cetshwayo, Sir Henry Bulwer was not co-operative. Chelmsford wrote to Frere, 'He is, I think, a very self-opiniated man, ... But he has essentially a small mind and cannot take a full grasp of the situation. ... He wishes to settle every petty point of detail himself. He is very particular about the exact language in which his orders are clothed, and will discuss and alter *ad nauseam* every sentence. On the other hand he

* 2/3rd, 1/13th, 2/24th and 90th were complete. 1/24th was without 3 companies still mopping up the Kaffir war in Cape Province. The garrison of the Cape was 88th Foot which sent one company to Natal.

61

has very good abilities . . . and a very keen desire to gain a reputation for strict justice.' Fortunately for Chelmsford news arrived in mid-September that 'Cetshwayo had ordered two of his strongest regiments to assemble in the neighbourhood of the Tugela for the ostensible purpose of a hunt [although] there is no game in that part of Zululand'. This induced Sir Henry to 'send out a warning to the several magistrates along the border', and to call a meeting of the Natal Defence Committee. After some deliberation the Committee decided to purchase a thousand Enfield rifles 'but these cannot be made available for some time, as they are scattered about in different merchants' stores all over the country. No provision has been made for the supply of ammunition.' Late in October another report announced that Cetshwayo had concentrated his army at Ulundi and this news persuaded the Lieutenant-Governor to call out the Volunteers and to consent to the raising of units of native troops under white officers.

From the Transvaal there was a minimum of assistance, the Boers feeling that since Britain insisted on extending her protection to their republic the British could do the work of defending them. One small unit of forty men was raised by a border farmer with good reasons for hating the Zulus and one Krupp gun was unearthed from the government stores in Pretoria. The rest of the Boers gave nothing but good advice. In particular, they urged Chelmsford not to neglect laagering his wagons when he halted. This advice was sound but impractical. Laagering was a difficult and peculiarly Boer skill. None of them could be induced to accompany the army as laager commandants.

The entire force, including the skeletal garrisons which had to be left in Natal and the Transvaal consisted of 16,000 fighting men, of whom more than 9,000 were hastily raised and poorly armed natives and 1,100 were colonial volunteers, all of them mounted. Included in the total was a naval brigade of 170 sailors and marines who brought with them two 12 pounders on field carriages and a gatling gun.

Working on the assumption that the conquest of Zululand would take six weeks, it was estimated that 1,800 tons of stores would be required. Rations and ammunition for the whole force would have to be brought up from the colonies as there was no prospect of being able to acquire any substantial quantity of food in Zululand, except slaughter cattle which travelled on the hoof and presented no serious transport problem. Natal was scoured for wagons and teams. Hiring was difficult and most had to be bought at inflated prices. By January, 1879, Chelmsford and his staff had managed to acquire 977 wagons, 56 carts, 10,023 oxen, 803 horses and 398 mules. To manage this mass of transport 2,000 additional natives had to be hired.

There remained the problem of how to conquer Zululand. The principles of war would demand a single overwhelming thrust, the concentration of force. This, however, would lay Natal open to exactly the kind of disaster which the invasion was designed to prevent. If the whole monstrous convoy of more than a thousand vehicles plodded its way along one of the few tracks that led into the interior, half of Cetshwayo's army would be sufficient to harass and delay it while 20,000 warriors would still be available to raid into defenceless Natal. Believing that a number of strong self-contained forces crossing into Zululand at widely different points would occupy the attention of most, if not all, the enemy forces, Chelmsford decided to divide the army and launch concentric attacks on the capital, Ulundi.

There were only two passable tracks into Zululand from Natal. On the east the Tugela can be crossed near its mouth, Lower Tugela Drift, and a track runs to Ulundi by way of Eshowe and the mission station of St Paul's. At the other end of the border, a hundred and fifty miles away by road, there was another track to the capital which crosses the Buffalo at Rorke's Drift and ran eastward by way of Isandhlwana mountain.

Between these two routes the road north-east from Greytown ran down to the Tugela at Middle Drift. This crossing place had been constructed in 1875 by Wolseley with a view to an invasion of Zululand. Unfortunately Sir Garnet had not thought his plan through. 'The country on the opposite side of the river is exceedingly broken, and although Bishop Schroeder, the Norwegian missionary, did once contrive to bring a wagon from his mission station at Entumeni, via Middle Drift, into Natal, an invasion of Zululand at that point would have been impossible.' It was pointless to use this route since the track, such as it was, led to Eshowe which could be reached more easily by way of Lower Tugela Drift.

From the Transvaal a track ran east from Utrecht and crossed the Blood River at a very difficult drift about thirty-five miles north of Rorke's Drift.

Chelmsford decided on a three-pronged advance, one on each of the practicable routes. Each of the attacking columns contained two British regular battalions.* Another, consisting entirely of native levies and a rocket battery, was to march to Middle Drift in the hope of convincing the enemy that a fourth advance was contemplated. There was also a fifth force which included a regular battalion. This was stationed in the south-eastern Transvaal with its base at Luneberg, north of the Pongola river. Its stated purpose was to assist in the defence of the Transvaal. It served also as a check on any Boer extremists who might attempt to re-establish independence while the British attention was fixed on Zululand.

The decision to disperse his attacking force into three columns was a difficult one for Chelmsford to take. It exposed him to much malicious criticism from his contemporaries when setbacks occurred and has made him the butt of armchair strategists ever since. His problem was to defeat the Zulu army and take the Zulu capital in a short sharp campaign while at the same time preventing an army greatly superior to his own in numbers and mobility from counterattacking into Natal or the Transvaal. No track in Zululand could stand the passage of 18,000 men and 1,000 vehicles without total reconstruction which was impossible in the

* One battalion, (99th Foot, less one company) in the right hand column had just landed at Durban from England.

time available. By dividing his strength he reduced the possibility of a counter-strike to a minimum and greatly increased the potential speed of his own advances. He believed that superior fire power could compensate for the enemy's advantages in numbers and mobility, that two battalions of regulars each with the colonial equivalent of four squadrons of cavalry could drive off any attack the Zulus could make upon it, provided that their supply of ammunition was assured. The experience of two of the three columns showed that he was right but in the third his theory was not proof against the blunders of his subordinates.

Just before the invasion started he wrote to the Duke of Cambridge, 'Our movements will all be made in the most deliberate manner. There is nothing to be gained by a rapid forward movement and, if I wished to make a rush, I should be unable to carry it out, consequent upon the great difficulty of supply and transport. We are now in the most rainy season of the year and convoys are sadly delayed by the state of the roads.'

Frere's ultimatum expired at midnight on 10 January, 1879. Already the left and right columns had established bridgeheads on the Zulu banks of the rivers. In the centre the entire column was encamped around the mission house near Rorke's Drift. The column's commander was Brevet Lieutenant-Colonel Glyn of the Twenty-Fourth Foot but Lord Chelmsford and his staff were accompanying that column and they rode into camp on the day before the ultimatum ran out. Glyn may have felt some resentment at the presence of the commander-in-chief with his force but it is unlikely that he was greatly upset. Chelmsford was immensely popular with all ranks. 'He was,' wrote one of the officers, 'always a man with a kind heart, beloved by his soldiers and loving them in return.' Since his successful campaign in the Transkei in the previous year they also had confidence in his ability. 'From under a rather low white helmet, his anxious face peered out; a nose long and thin and, if anything, hooked; the principal features black, bushy eyebrows from under which his dark eyes seemed to move restlessly, ever on the watch for something sudden coming. A pleasant manner, sharp, rather jerky sentences, and a general air of watchfulness pervading all his actions. He walked quickly, turning his head from side to side, and stopping frequently to remark on some arrangement which required attention.' He inspected the native regiment that was with the column and 'seemed much pleased with them, and addressed them, saying that no prisoners, women or children were to be injured in any way.'

Reveille was sounded at 2 am the next morning. The weather was clear but soon 'a thick mist came on, accompanied by drizzling rain'. By half past four the tents had been struck and Colonel Harness's battery of six 7 pounders were unlimbered on some rising ground to cover the river crossing. The first troops across were a battalion of the Natal Native Contingent. The drift was 'broad, deep and with a heavy current, but there was a small island in the centre which helped to facilitate the transit.' The water 'came up to the men's necks in places' and a few were swept away and drowned. Next, a cable was hauled across and one of the prefabricated ponts was secured to the end. The mounted men put their carbines in the pont and rode, unarmed, a short distance upstream where they crossed at a deep ford. Their carbines were hauled across and reissued to them. Then they trotted forward to a ridge of high ground and deployed as a screen of vedettes. By this time the second pont had been harnessed and, using the two boats, the two British battalions, 1st and 2nd Twenty-Fourth Foot, were slowly ferried across. There was still a thick mist and as the regulars arrived on the far bank they were disposed in a defensive perimeter, three miles long. Not a shot was fired but when the mist lifted an armed Zulu was seen guarding a herd. The Zulu and his cattle were promptly captured by mounted troops.

Having seen his bridgehead secure, Lord Chelmsford rode through the outpost line with a small escort. Moving north he met the commander of the left-hand column, Colonel Evelyn Wood V.C., at a previously arranged rendezvous. It was obvious that the Zulus were surprised by the prompt British move. Wood told how his column had seized a large number of cattle grazing near the river. When he asked the Zulus guarding them why they had not driven them into the interior, he got the reply, 'Oh, we never thought you would begin on the day you mentioned.'

Next day a small striking force was detached to seize the kraal of a chief called Sihayo. It had been two of Sihayo's wives who had fled to Natal and been seized and killed by a party led by some of his sons. Since the conduct of his family had been the immediate *casus belli*, a prompt punishment for them was a political necessity. The seizure of his stock cost a brisk skirmish in which the Native Contingent suffered sixteen casualties but at the end of the day 13 horses, 413 cattle, 332 goats and 235 sheep were in British hands.

When the main force started its advance, Chelmsford's wisdom in not attempting to move his whole army on a single track was immediately apparent. As the Official History of the war remarked, 'although footpaths and cattle tracks led through Zululand, roads did not exist. The only wheeled transport which had previously traversed this region was the wagon of an occasional trader or sportsman, and the old grass-covered ruts which these had left were the sole guides in selecting the route for the line of advance.' The centre column alone had 220 wagons. Each of them was eighteen feet long and was dragged by eight or nine pair of oxen. The load on each could be as much as four ton. The passage of such a convoy would wreck a better track than any in Zululand and to make matters worse the country, as Chelmsford reported, 'is in a terrible state from the rain'. There were daily thunderstorms which an experienced officer described as 'the worst I have ever seen anywhere, and a dry spruit would in an hour or so become a raging torrent 12 or even 20 feet deep.'

The only professional assistance in building the track for

the centre column consisted of a lieutenant and four sappers of the Royal Engineers and a lieutenant and ten privates of the Natal Native Pioneer Corps. Most of the work had to be done by the infantry, British and native. In the circumstances it was a considerable feat of organization that on 20 January, nine days after the advance had started, the bulk of the column reached a camp site at the foot of Isandhlwana hill. This was six and a half miles from Rorke's Drift in a straight line but more than nine miles by the track. Much of the transport could not get as far on that day and had to be encamped along the track with small infantry escorts.

There was no prospect of a further advance for several days. The wagons would have to be unloaded, the stores stacked and guarded while the transport went back to the depot at Rorke's Drift to ferry forward more supplies to Isandhlwana, the first of a series of advance supply dumps for the further advance. The heavy rain was making it almost as difficult to move wheeled transport within Natal as it was in Zululand.

In fact, the delay would be advantageous. There was a chance that the weather might dry out and it would only be a few days before one of the Engineer companies sent out from England would have marched up from Durban and joined the column, thus greatly easing the road-building difficulties. With them would come three more companies of the Twenty-Fourth Foot. These had been left in Natal, two at Helpmakaar, one at Rorke's Drift, to guard the lines of communication until they could be relieved by the 2nd Battalion the King's Own who had arrived in the colony with the sappers.

CHAPTER 6

Counterstrike

The day after the centre column reached Isandhlwana, Chelmsford sent out a reconnaisance in force to the southeast. Major Dartnell was in command and he had with him sixteen companies of the Natal Native Contingent and the bulk of the mounted troops. Towards the end of the day he sent back a number of messages saying that Zulus were around in large numbers. A final message, which reached camp at 2 am on the morning of 22 January, pleaded for infantry reinforcements so that he could attack. Chelmsford was hoping for an early battle so that he could discourage them by inflicting a sharp defeat on them. He decided to support Dartnell by joining him with six companies of the 2nd battalion, the Twenty-Fourth, his only squadron of mounted infantry and four out of Harness's six 7 pounders. The only wheeled transport accompanying the force was the artillery limbers since it was important to keep the troops as mobile as possible. The infantry had one hundred rounds each in their ammunition pouches. The force moved off as soon as daylight broke and the camp, with the convoy of wagons, was left in the charge of Brevet Lieutenant-Colonel Henry Burmester Pulleine.

Pulleine had recently passed his fortieth birthday. Like many army officers he was the son of a Church of England rector although his grandfather had commanded the Scots Greys. Educated at Marlborough he had gone to Sandhurst from which he had emerged with a free commission as an ensign in the Thirtieth Foot shortly before his seventeenth birthday. Three years later he was given a lieutenancy, without purchase, in the newly raised 2nd battalion of the Twenty-Fourth. As a subaltern he had seen service in Ireland, the Isles of Wight and Man, in Sheffield, Aldershot and Mauritius. Five years after his first commission he bought a captaincy in the same regiment and, eleven years later, a majority. In these higher ranks he served further afield, in India and Burma besides doing a short period on the Quartermaster-General's staff in Malta. He was a good staff officer with an understanding of supply problems having had a four year attachment to the Commissariat Department.

He was in his fifth year in South Africa but, although by 1879 he was senior major of the 1st battalion, the Twenty-Fourth, he had seen no active service. While his battalion had been engaged in the Transkei fighting he had been kept in staff appointments as town commandant first of Durban and later of King William's Town. He was good at this kind of work, having the knack, uncommon among regular officers, of getting on well with the colonials. He realized that he was at a disadvantage from never having seen a shot fired in anger and when a Zulu war seemed imminent petitioned Lord Chelmsford to be allowed to join his battalion. The General agreed and by hard riding Pulleine managed to catch up with the column on 17 January between Rorke's Drift and Isandhlwana.

Since his commanding officer, Colonel Glyn, the column commander, had ridden out with Chelmsford, command at the camp fell to Pulleine and it was a task for which he seemed, with his administrative experience, to be very suitable. His main occupation would have to be organizing the turn-round of the wagons prior to their return to Rorke's Drift.

His charge consisted of a camp for four and a half thousand men. Lines of bell-tents stood in shining white lines facing east across a plain. Behind the tents were the wagon lines containing more than two hundred of the huge wagons and fifteen hundred oxen. Behind them again rose, forbiddingly sheer, Isandhlwana hill, a rocky pile shaped like an elongated flowerpot. Its longer sides, those to the east and west, were impracticable for armed men, although its short, north and south, ends could be climbed, certainly by the agile, lightly-armed Zulus. Nevertheless, being easily defensible it was a valuable protection for the rear of the camp. Unfortunately the tent lines were too long to fit in front of the hill itself and projected to the south where their rear was covered by a small feature known as Stony Hill which was joined to the Isandhlwana massif by a pass, or nek, over which ran the track from Rorke's Drift.

When Colonel Glyn* had first laid out the camp he had chosen to assume that the whole line Isandhlwana—Stony Hill was impassable, which it clearly was not. He had posted no rearward defence to the camp. On the 20th the urgent representation of the field officer of the day had led him to post in the nek a piquet consisting of the officer and ten men of the Natal Native Pioneers who could give warning of an attack from the west. Glyn had, however, stationed his own battalion of the Twenty-Fourth at the south end of the line since they were the troops most able to stand an attack from three sides.

The east face of the camp was rather less than a thousand yards long and to defend it Pulleine had, apart from a swarm of unarmed transport drivers, about nine hundred soldiers. The hard corps of the garrison were five companies of his own battalion and one of the second battalion. Each company was about 75–80 strong. There were also the usual number of 'base details' from the two battalions, including the band of the 1st battalion, who were trained as stretcher bearers. The artillery consisted of only two 7 pounders but there were plenty of artillerymen, two officers and seventy gunners, since only minimal crews had gone out with the general. Nor were mounted men plentiful. All that had remained in camp were the piquets which had been on duty the

* Lord Chelmsford's critics have always held him responsible for the lay-out of the camp but, although there is no direct evidence either way, it seems from the General's character likely that he would have gone to great lengths to avoid breathing down the column commander's neck and would have left such arrangements to Glyn.

day before. There were 118 of them, including five officers and a number of sick.

The remainder of the garrison comprised four companies, drawn from two different battalions, of the Natal Native Contingent. No one had great confidence in these levies. They were sketchily trained and drawn from tribes in Natal which went in fear of the Zulus. Whatever their merits they were badly underarmed. Each company was supposed to consist of the European officers, six European NCOs and a hundred natives. All the Europeans and ten native NCOs in each company carried breech-loading rifles. Of the ninety remaining natives, a few carried ancient muzzle-loading fire-arms, a few carried bill-hooks but the majority were armed with shield and assegai. Even the shields were not the head-to-toe design carried by the Zulus but an inferior variety barely three feet long. The NNC companies made little contribution to the British firepower. From a strength of 420 all ranks, they could contribute the fire of sixty rifles. Pulleine, in fact, had a total rifle strength of little more than six hundred rifles, too few to defend the whole perimeter of the camp.

According to Field Force Regulations, the camp should have been entrenched but it would have been impracticable to do so. The ground was rocky and even to scrape a shallow shelter trench would have been at least a day's hard work for tired men. There was, in addition a shortage of tools for such work and such as were available were needed to improve the wagon track.

The Boers had strongly recommended that a laager should be formed. This entailed putting the wagons in a continuous formation, usually a circle, with the tow chains of one hooked on to the wagon in front. The oxen should be put inside the laager since the force would be immobilized if they were lost to the enemy. A very high degree of skill was required to form a laager and even the Boers found it difficult to achieve with untrained, native drivers. Moreover, the final move of each wagon had to be done by human strength, each of the loaded wagons needing about fifty men to roll it into position.

On 21 January the possibility of forming a laager had been mooted and Chelmsford had decided against it. If one was formed that evening it would have to be broken up again on the following morning since it was of the highest importance that the wagons should be unloaded and sent back to Natal for another consignment of stores. He also believed the position at the camp to be a strong one. He said later, 'There never was a position where a small force could have made a better defensive stand.' Pulleine's adjutant, Lieutenant Melvill, disagreed with him and said to Pulleine, 'The Zulus will charge home, and with our small numbers we ought to be in laager, or, at any rate, be prepared to stand shoulder to shoulder.'

Pulleine's orders, issued before Chelmsford left camp, were to draw in the line of defence while the General's force was out of camp; to keep a line of infantry piquets close to the camp; to send out a ring of mounted vedettes on the surrounding heights to give warning of a Zulu approach; to keep one wagon loaded with ammunition and ready to move up to replenish the troops on the reconnaissance. He was also told not to send wagons back to Rorke's Drift because there would not be enough men to escort them.

Pulleine sent out the whole of his mounted strength, except for the sick and a handful of mounted orderlies in a great semicircle from the north to the south but sent none out to the west. They were formed in small posts on hillocks about a mile from the camp. Four companies, two of NNC on the north, two of the Twenty-Fourth on the south, formed an inner ring near the camp. The piquet companies were deployed at the distances they would occupy in skirmishing order but the line was actually held by sentries while the soldiers rested by sections in the rear of their posts. They could have taken up their firing positions in less than two minutes. The small detachment of Natal Pioneers continued to guard the nek. They were better armed than the NNC infantry and each of the ten men had a Martini-Henry.

The reserve in camp consisted of four companies of 1st

Twenty-Fourth and two companies of NNC. From these a working party set out soon after dawn, under command of an officer of the Twenty-Fourth to continue the improvement of the track back to Natal. Pulleine recalled them at eight o'clock when he heard firing to the east which he assumed to be Chelmsford's force in action. Soon afterwards a messenger from one of the vedettes rode in with a report that a large force of Zulus could be seen to the north-east. Pulleine stood the whole garrison to arms, ordered the oxen to be secured and called in the two piquet companies of Twenty-Fourth since that side did not seem to be threatened. He then sent off an orderly to Chelmsford with a message which read, 'Report just come in that Zulus are advancing in force from left front of camp'. Having taken all reasonable precautions, he settled down to wait for further news. Isolated groups of Zulus were occasionally glimpsed on the skyline about two miles to the north-east and the vedettes reported others, as far or further away to the west.

It is unlikely that Pulleine was greatly worried about an attack on the camp as he was expecting to be reinforced during the morning by a substantial body of troops under an officer senior to himself. Before leaving camp that morning Lord Chelmsford had sent Lieutenant Smith-Dorrien to call up the column which had earlier been ordered to demonstrate around Middle Drift.

This column consisted of three battalions of NNC, a unit of mounted natives (270 men known as Sikali's Horse) and a Royal Artillery Rocket battery. Their commander, Colonel Durnford, had not relished the passive role of demonstrating at the Drift and had been on the point of undertaking an unauthorized foray into Zululand when he was halted by an unusually sharp note from Chelmsford which opened, 'Unless you carry out the instructions I give you, it will be my unpleasant duty to remove you from your command.' Subsequently he had been ordered to move the whole of his column, less one battalion, to Rorke's Drift.

Anthony William Durnford was born in 1830, the son of an officer of Royal Engineers who had risen to be a general.

He had gone to Woolwich and been commissioned into his father's corps in 1848. He had served in Ceylon, Malta and Gibraltar and would have gone to China if he had not been struck down with heat apoplexy on the voyage out. He had been in South Africa since 1872 and knew the Zulus better than any other British officer. He had attended Cetshwayo's enthronement as one of Shepstone's entourage and had been a member of Bulwer's boundary commission. He was a close friend of the Colenso family and Natal rumour had it that he was engaged to one of the bishop's daughters although he had a wife in England whose existence seems to have been unknown in Pietermaritzburg. In the fighting in the Transkei he had gained a reputation for bravery and his left arm had been disabled by an assegai thrust. He had also acquired a reputation, probably justified, for rashness. He had been put in charge of the raising of the Natal Native Contingent and the NNC were said to be prepared to do things for him they would do for no other officer.

His orders from Chelmsford on the morning of 22 January were explicit. 'You are to march to this camp [Isandhlwana] at once with all the force you have with you.

'2/24th, artillery and mounted men, with the general, move off at once to attack a Zulu force about ten miles distant.

'If Bengough's [detached] battalion [of NNC] has crossed the river at Eland's Drift, it is to move up here.'

There could be no doubt about the meaning of these orders, whatever may have been said of them later. Durnford was to take all his troops, including the battalion which had previously been detached, to Isandhlwana to make up the strength of the garrison, depleted by Chelmsford's foray to the east. It followed that he would take over the command at the camp since he was three years senior to Pulleine as a lieutenant-colonel by brevet.* In addition he had recently been sharply reminded by Chelmsford of the need for ex-

---

* The *London Gazette* had carried his appointment as colonel by brevet dated 11 December, 1878, but it is unlikely that the news had reached him.

plicit obedience to orders.

He arrived at the camp at 10.30 am, accompanied by Sikhali's Horse. Three companies of NNC were following as fast as they could march, escorting three rocket troughs and ten wagons carrying his column's stores and reserve ammunition. Since all his horsemen were fully armed with Martini-Henry rifles, the gain to the firepower of the garrison would, including the officers and NCOs of the NNC companies, be about 300 badly needed rifles. However, when Pulleine attempted to hand over command of the camp, Durnford blithely announced that he and his men would not be staying.

He immediately sent out his horsemen to clear a few isolated groups of Zulus from the high ground to the north of the camp. This was a reasonable operation, if hardly essential, and Pulleine agreed to support it by strengthening the northern end of his piquet line by relieving a NNC company with E Company 1st Twenty-Fourth under Lieutenant Cavaye on a spur immediately north of the camp. The remaining troops, except for sentries, were fallen out to get their mid-day meal. They were not allowed to take off their equipment.

Durnford and Pulleine took an early lunch, soon after eleven, and while they were eating, the observation post on top of Isandhlwana hill reported that a body of about five hundred Zulus, which had been lurking to the north-east was moving away eastward.

Disregarding his orders, Durnford decided to follow them on the pretext of preventing them from joining their fellows who were opposing Lord Chelmsford. Since he intended taking out a force of all arms, it is hard to see how he expected to intercept a body of fast-moving warriors who already had three miles start on him. In an appalling display of irresponsibility he asked Pulleine to give him two companies of the Twenty-Fourth, a third of the reliable infantry in camp, as a support. Pulleine replied that his orders were to defend the camp and that he did not feel justified in making such a detachment. Durnford continued to press him and eventually he gave way and said, 'Oh, very well. If you order them, I'll give you them.'

Pulleine gave orders to his adjutant to get the two companies ready to march but Melvill objected strongly. He had much more experience of active service than Pulleine and induced him to change his mind. Melvill then went to Durnford and said, 'Colonel, I really do not think Colonel Pulleine would be doing right to send any men out of camp when his orders are to defend the camp.' Durnford replied 'Very well, it does not much matter; we will not take them.' However, before riding out he said to Pulleine that he would expect support if he got into difficulties.

Soon after 11.30 he cantered out of camp with two of the five troops of Sikhali's Horse, ordering one company of NNC to follow with the rocket troughs. They moved due east and the mounted men were soon out of sight behind a conical hill on which Pulleine had posted a vedette about a mile from the camp.

While Durnford's marching troops with the rockets were still in sight from the camp there was an alarm from the north. The two troops of Sikhali's Horse which he had sent to sweep the high ground on the left flank of the camp had found nothing but, without orders, had pushed on into the valley beyond. To their astonishment they almost rode into a whole Zulu regiment, about 4,000 men, concealed in a ravine. They fell back in good order with the Zulus in pursuit. The horsemen retired by troops in succession, covering each other by fire, but their musketry could not halt the Zulus. Soon after noon they sent back Captain George Shepstone, one of Theophilus' sons, to ask Pulleine for reinforcements.

At almost the same time, the vedette on Conical Hill sent down a warning to Durnford, now four miles from camp, that an immense impi was hiding on his left and could cut him off from the camp. The Colonel ignored the warning, merely sending back a message that he would count on the support of the vedette if he was attacked.

Hardly had he sent this message when a large number of Zulus in loose order swept over the skyline about 1,500 yards

77

to his left front. Even then he did not order a retreat. He dismounted his men, deployed them and waited until the enemy were within four hundred yards before opening fire. The rifles did not halt the onrush. Only about eighty men were firing,* all of them Africans, and the enemy outnumbered them by twenty or thirty to one. He ordered first one troop and then the other to retire and took up a new position near Conical Hill and his rockets and their escorting company swung into line on his left, next to the hill.

While Durnford's action was developing, at about 12.15, Captain Gardner, 14th Hussars, one of Glyn's staff officers, rode into camp with a message from Chelmsford. This told Pulleine to strike camp and bring the garrison with the wagons to join the rest of the force at a new site twelve miles further on. Gardner's arrival coincided with that of George Shepstone from the left flank. After a moment's hesitation Pulleine decided that he could not obey. He replied in a hurried note, 'Heavy firing to the left of our camp. Cannot move camp at present.' Before this was despatched Gardner added, perhaps at Pulleine's request, 'Heavy firing near left of our camp. Shepstone has come in for reinforcements and reports Basutos falling back. The whole force at camp turned out and fighting about one mile to its left flank.'

Pulleine had all the troops called to their arms and sent the fifth and last troop of Sikhali's Horse to reinforce their comrades on the high ground. To support them one of Durnford's companies of NNC was marched to the north. Behind them a second company of the Twenty-Fourth was sent to strengthen Cavaye on the spur. The available reserve now consisted of four regular companies, two of NNC, two guns and about thirty colonial horsemen. The spare files of the Twenty-Fourth were hastily improvised into an extra company.

As these dispositions were being made, heavy firing started to be heard from the direction of Conical Hill. It was obvious

---

* The two troops numbered rather more than a hundred men but when fighting dismounted one man in five would be needed as horse-holders.

that Durnford was heavily engaged and the fact that his rocket launchers each fired once but once only suggested that he was in serious trouble for the fusilade continued unabated. Pulleine was now in a terrible dilemma. He was under heavy attack from the north and his first duty was to defend the camp. He knew, and Melvill would have reminded him, that he could only succeed with his men in close formation. On the other hand he had Durnford's order to support him if he ran into trouble. It was an order incompatible with his prime responsibility but it was unthinkable to abandon Durnford without making an effort to rescue him. He decided to extend his line of battle from the spur to the north of the camp occupied by Cavaye's company on the left to Conical Hill on the right. The latter flank would be in the air but he counted on Durnford's men to secure it. It was a disastrous decision. Durnford, who had set up the situation, should have been left to make the best retreat he could from the consequences of his own folly and disobedience. Nevertheless it is hard to dissent from Pulleine's determination to try to extricate his superior officer.

In front of the new line of battle, the Zulus could make no progress. On the spur where Mostyn's company reinforced Cavaye's, the men were comfortably lying behind cover in extended order. The Zulu regiment which attacked them took so many casualties that it broke and fled over the skyline. Along the rest of the front the warriors were driven to ground in the dry watercourses which laced the ground. Smith-Dorrien, who was in the rear of the line, wrote that 'The Twenty-Fourth were no boy recruits, but war-worn, matured men, mostly with beards, and fresh from a long campaign in the old [Cape] colony where they had carried everything before them. Possessed of a splendid discipline and sure of success, they lay in their position making every round tell.'

Each man carried a hundred rounds in his pouches but these would not last for ever. The NNC infantry were seen to be blazing away 'at an absurd rate'. There was plenty of ammunition in camp and there a scratch collection of

79

'artillerymen in charge of spare horses, officers' servants, sick, etc' were organized into parties breaking open the ammunition boxes, which were screwed down so that 'it was a very difficult task to get them open', and taking them to the men in the firing line. There were some minor disputes as quartermasters tried to get their own ammunition for their own battalions, but the supply never faltered. The problem was to get ammunition to the men at the far, eastern end of the line, almost a mile from the camp. One mule-cart load was delivered but those on the extreme right flank were soon short.

Pulleine's gallant but misguided effort to rescue Durnford was ill-requited. The remaining thirty horsemen had ridden out to reinforce Durnford but the colonel, seeing himself outflanked, decided on a rapid retreat to the camp. Thus while Pulleine was stretching out his right to get in touch with Durnford, Durnford was no longer there and Pulleine's flank was in the air. He had no alternative to ordering the companies to retire in succession, hoping to take up the close order position round the camp which they should never have left.

It was too late. The line Pulleine had formed had broken the Zulu 'chest' but the two 'horns' swung wide. The left 'horn' passed south of Conical Hill and its extreme tip reached the camp as the regulars were falling back on it. A great mass of warriors struck in from the south-east. They came on 'giving vent to no loud war-cries, but to a low musical murmuring noise, which gave the impression of a gigantic swarm of bees getting nearer and nearer'. They suffered losses which would have crippled a European army. Some Zulu units were forced to go to ground but there were too many to be stopped.

In the camp there was pandemonium. 'All the transport drivers, panic-stricken,¹ were jostling each other with their teams and wagons, shouting and yelling at their cattle, and striving to get over the Nek on to the Rorke's Drift road.' They were joined in their flight by many of the Natal Native Contingent, including not a few of their European officers and sergeants. Those who managed to get over the nek found no safety. The right 'horn' of the Zulu attack had trotted round behind Isandhlwana hill and blocked the road. The only escape route was to the south and even that gap was soon closed.

At the camp there could only be one end to the fighting. It had been Pulleine's last tenuous hope that the remainder of the regulars with the remnants of the colonial horsemen could fight with their backs to their ammunition supply until the Zulu fighting spirit was broken by their losses. It was not to be. The simultaneous arrival of the Zulus and the troops in the camp meant that the Twenty-Fourth were broken up into isolated groups, none larger than a company. There was no future in surrendering to Zulus and the men fought on as long as their ammunition lasted. Then they used their bayonets against the heavy assegais until, in the end, they were overpowered.

As soon as it was certain that the battle was lost, Pulleine ordered Melvill, who being adjutant was mounted, to take the Queen's Colour and try to escape. Escorted by Lieutenant Coghill, who had wrenched his knee and had to be mounted, Melvill carried the precious Colour as far as the Buffalo River. There their mounts were shot by the pursuing Zulus and both men were assegaied. The Colour was thrown into the river.

At the camp the struggling islands of scarlet were flooded one by one by the irresistible black tide. The last group of all were sixty men of Captain Younghusband's company. It made a final stand high on the southern face of Isandhlwana hill. At last, when they had fired their last rounds, they made a despairing charge downhill led by Younghusband, whirling his sword round his head. They had no hope and chose to die as a body rather than be hacked down one by one. One man only escaped and he climbed the hill and established himself in a small cave. With his rear protected and a few rounds of ammunition, he lay there, fighting off the Zulus until he was shot through the head. Pulleine and Durnford had died earlier, fighting close to each other at the eastern foot of the nek.

At about five o'clock silence finally fell over the battlefield. The Zulus gave themselves over to an orgy of destruction. The tents and stores were comprehensively plundered. The transport oxen, the horses and the wounded were slaughtered. The bellies of the dead, human and animal, were slit open lest, according to Zulu belief, they should become the abode of evil spirits. Some of the warriors refreshed themselves from the rum casks. One unwisely tried drinking a bottle of carbolic from Surgeon-Major Shephard's medical stores. So intent were the warriors that they scarcely noticed when a sick officer on a tired pony rode into the camp from Chelmsford's force. He realized his mistake, turned about and spurred his tired pony away to the east. Only a few scattered shots followed him.

At noon there had been sixteen officers and 409 other ranks of the 1st battalion of the Twenty-Fourth Foot in camp.* Two bandsmen and a groom were still alive by evening. The second battalion had numbered five officers and 178 men.† There were no survivors. The mounted troops did not fare quite so badly. Forty-three outlived the day. Their horses made it easier for them to escape. Some left before and some after the situation became desperate. Ten artillerymen survived. About half of the men in the ranks of the Natal Native Contingent got away, since some companies disintegrated before the Zulu 'horns' closed. The combined strength of the forces of Durnford and Pulleine was 1,774 all ranks. That evening they had left 1,329 corpses in and around the camp and on the track to Fugitives' Drift on the Buffalo.

Chelmsford's invasion was brought to a sharp halt. He had lost half his reliable infantry and all his transport. All that stood between the Zulus and the long-feared invasion of Natal was Lieutenant Chard and the tiny garrison of Rorke's Drift.

---

* Including men detached to the mounted infantry, rocket battery, and force headquarters.

CHAPTER 7

The Oscarberg Mission House

Half a mile from Rorke's Drift, where Chard and his party were working on the ponts, B Company, 2nd battalion, Twenty-Fourth Foot were encamped around the pair of buildings which had once been Jim Rorke's farm and were now the Oscarberg Mission. As the only buildings near the drift they had been requisitioned as a base hospital and supply depot for the centre column. B Company had been left as a temporary garrison until the King's Own could march up from Durban and relieve them. The men were not pleased at being left behind and looked forward to the day when they could go forward and join their battalion. On the morning of 22 January the company felt secure. Routine sentries were posted and a few men were on fatigues. The rest of the men were idling about their tents.

Soon after midday the thud of 7 pounders could be heard away to the east. One man in camp did not hear them. The company commander, Lieutenant Gonville Bromhead, although only thirty-three was becoming so deaf that he could not hear orders on parade.* He came from a long line of soldiers. His great-grandfather, a colonel, had had four

---

* In his despatch Lord Chelmsford referred to Chard and Bromhead as 'two young officers'. They were both over thirty. Subsequent accounts tend to speak of them as mere striplings. The fact that Chelmsford could speak of lieutenants in their thirties as being young is a commentary on an army in which promotion went almost entirely by seniority. Sixty-six years earlier, William Napier (who was not a purchasing officer) was lamenting that 'I cannot rise to the head of my profession for want of time ... I am 28 and only a major.'

brothers in the army, one of whom was killed at Falkirk in
1746. His grandfather had distinguished himself on Burgoyne's campaign but had been captured at Saratoga. He
died a lieutenant-general and a baronet. His father fought as
a lieutenant at Waterloo but the outstanding Bromhead of
that generation had been a cousin who commanded the
Seventy-Seventh when, with the Fifth Foot, they had advanced uphill in line against French cavalry and routed them
at El Bodon. Two of Gonville Bromhead's brothers were in
the army. One had fought in the Crimea, another, a favourite
of Wolseley's, had distinguished himself in the Ashanti campaign. The family also had academic connections and the
company commander's unusual Christian name recalled
his great-grandfather's marriage into the family of the co-
founders of Gonville and Caius College, Cambridge.

Bromhead was not alarmed when the gunfire was reported
to him. Some firing to the east was to be expected and there
was a large body of troops between the Buffalo and the Zulu
armies. Isandhlwana was only six miles as the crow flies
from Rorke's Drift but the intervening hills muffled the
sound of musketry from the beleaguered camp.* If it had
been possible to hear how desperate the fighting was, Bromhead might not have been so willing to allow three men from
the camp to ride up Oscarberg Hill, east of the mission, to
see if there was anything to be seen.

The three men were Surgeon-Major Reynolds, in charge
of the hospital, the Reverend George Smith, a missionary
who had joined the army as a temporary chaplain, and the
Reverend Otto Witt, who had charge of the Oscarberg
mission. Witt had sent his wife and their three young children
off to Pietermaritzberg a few days earlier but had stayed
behind to look after the mission property. Since his house
was being used as the hospital, Bromhead had lent him a
tent and he had been making himself useful by acting as an
interpreter between the surgeon major and his Kaffir orderlies.

*The hills seem also to have made the cannon fire inaudible to Chard
and his party working at the drift.

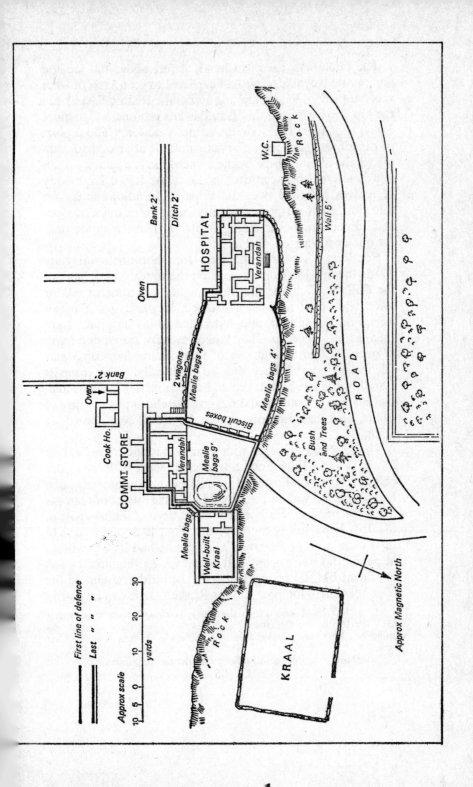

First line of defence

Last " " "

Approx scale

10 5 0 10 20 30
yards

Approx Magnetic North

Bank 2'
Ditch 2'

W.C.

Rock

Wall 5'

ROAD

Bush and Trees

HOSPITAL

Verandah

Oven

2 wagons

Mealie bags 4'

Mealie bags 4'

Biscuit boxes

Bank 2'

Oven

Cook Ho.

COMMI STORE

Verandah

Mealie bags 9'

Mealie bags

Well-built Kraal

Rock

KRAAL

The Oscarberg rises five hundred feet above the mission and, wrote Reynolds, 'we had expected to get a view of what was happening, but on looking across the Buffalo River from the top we discovered that Isandhlwana mountain (five miles away) shut from our view the scene of action.* The reports of three more guns were distinctly audible after we had completed the ascent, there being, I should say, a quarter of an hour's interval between each of them. At 1.30 a large body of natives marched over the slope of Isandhlwana in our direction, their purpose evidently being to examine ravines and ruined kraals for hiding fugitives. These men we took for our own Native Contingent.'

Not long afterwards they saw four horsemen riding towards the mission from the east on the south, Natal, bank of the Buffalo. Thinking that they might have come to ask for some additional medical assistance, Reynolds left the two clerics on the summit and rode back to his hospital. 'I got there as they rode up. They looked awfully scared and I was at once startled to find one of them riding Surgeon-Major Shephard's pony.† They shouted frantically. "The camp at Isandhlwana has been taken and all our men in it massacred, that no power could stand against the enormous number of Zulus, and that the only chance for us all was immediate flight." '

The four men brought with them a message from Captain Essex, Seventy-Fifth Foot, a transport officer with the centre column. Essex had escaped from the camp on his horse and had fought his way to Fugitives' Drift, five miles downstream from the mission. He had seen a number of Zulus cross at the drift in pursuit of the survivors. They had soon retired to their own bank of the river. The note he had hastily written in pencil did not suggest that an attack on the mission was imminent but, taken together with the lurid accounts of the four horsemen, the prospect for Rorke's Drift was an alarm-

* In a 'first hand' account to the *Daily Telegraph* Witt claimed that from the top of the Oscarberg 'we had an excellent view of what was going on'. Witt was as unreliable as a witness as he was in every other way.

† Shephard was the medical officer with the centre column.

ing one.

'War' remarked James Wolfe, before storming the heights of Abraham, 'is an option of difficulties,' and few junior officers have been faced with more difficult options than was Bromhead at that moment. He had not even time to consult his senior officer, Chard, down at the drift. Should B Company stand and fight where it was or should he try to break away and join the other two companies of the regiment in the more defensible post at Helpmakaar?

The dump of supplies and ammunition under his charge would be essential to whatever remained of the centre column. If he decided on retreat all would have to be abandoned. There were no wagons to carry them if there had been time and labour to load them. In the hospital were thirty-six wounded and sick, most of them incapable of marching. If the Zulus gave them time, the invalids could be put on to the two wagons available but whether the slow-moving wagons could cover the ten miles to Helpmakaar before the impis overtook them was quite another matter. It was quite certain that a hundred fit men would be too few to protect the wagons from a heavy attack in open country. Bromhead, and every man with him, never doubted for a moment that the Zulus, having shattered the troops opposed to them, would press on into Natal.

On the other hand, the defence of the mission station was a most unpromising undertaking. Another officer who knew the place commented that 'a worse position could hardly be imagined. Two small thatched buildings, about thirty-nine yards apart, with thin walls, commanded by rising ground on the south and west, and completely overlooked in the south by a high hill [the Oscarberg]. On the north side an orchard and garden gave good cover to within a few yards of the houses.'

Bromhead could have no idea how large a force might attack him—the number could be as great as ten thousand, it might even be more. He did know that his company consisted, apart from himself, of one colour-sergeant, four sergeants, one lance-sergeant, four corporals, three lance-corporals, sixty-eight private soldiers and two drummers. There was also a company of the Natal Native Contingent, one hundred strong. Their commander, Captain George Stephenson, and his handful of European NCOs could do little with them. They impressed the men of the Twenty-Fourth as sullen, shifty and thoroughly unreliable.

The presence of this company was only an embarrassment to Bromhead. Since they were untrustworthy the simplest solution would have been to order them to march away to Helpmakaar. Unfortunately this was impossible. For one thing, Stephenson, a captain even if only a colonial captain, might refuse to obey. Major Spalding had ordered him to serve under Chard but he had no orders to obey Bromhead. It woud be unlikely that he would be anxious to undertake a ten-mile march through Zulu-infested country with a hundred untried and unsupported Kaffirs. Even if he would agree, it was politically unthinkable to send the NNC out on their own. If they were caught and massacred, Bromhead would be held responsible, however practical his motives.

If the NNC were to stay and assist in the defence they posed another problem, quite apart from their reliability. Two hundred fighting men could not be crammed into a space which, with the sick and stores, would be convenient for one hundred. If they stayed the hospital would have to be included in the defensive perimeter. This meant that more fortifications would have to be built and there would not be men available to evacuate the sick from the hospital. Even if they were moved, they would have to lie in the open since the more solidly constructed store house was crammed with sacks and packing cases.

Bromhead's first move was to send a man down to the drift to warn Chard of the danger. Next he ordered the tents to be struck by the simple expedient of pulling away the centre pole. This not only cleared the field of fire but created a tangled mass of canvas, guy ropes and tent pegs which must impede an attacker. Then he consulted the Surgeon-Major and Assistant Commissary James Langley Dalton. Dalton, who was in his fifties, had been a sergeant in the Eighty-Fifth.

He had retired with a pension and settled in Natal. He had volunteered for the Commissariat service when war seemed imminent. At that moment he was invaluable for, during his service, he had done a course in field fortification. It was Dalton who traced out the line for a rampart and Bromhead set his men to building it on the plan the Commissary indicated.

Building material was plentiful. The store house was full of useful objects. One of the private soldiers who heaved them into place wrote that, 'The mealie bags were good heavy things, weighing about two hundred pounds each. The biscuit boxes contained ordinary army biscuit. They were big, square, wooden boxes, weighing about a hundredweight each. The meat boxes, too, were very heavy, as they contained tinned meat. They were smaller than the biscuit boxes.'

Chard received Bromhead's message while he was talking to Adendorff and Vane. He sent both men to Bromhead with orders to fortify the post. Sergeant Vane he instructed to ride on to Helpmakaar with the news of their danger. Chard stayed at the drift for a few minutes giving orders for the ponts to be moored in midstream. He also told Sergeant Milne to fill the watercart, to load the tools onto a nearby wagon and bring cart and wagon up to the mission. Then he mounted and galloped the half mile up the track to find that 'Lieutenant Bromhead was already most actively engaged in loopholing and barricading the store building and hospital, and also in connecting the defence of the two buildings by walls constructed with mealie bags and wagons. I held a hurried consultation with him and Mr Dalton of the Commissariat—who was actively superintending the work of the defence and whom I cannot sufficiently thank for his most valuable services, and I entirely approved of all his arrangements.'

While Chard was making his arrangements, Adendorff slipped quietly away. He decided that the news would be better carried to Helpmakaar and beyond by two men. He therefore reconsidered an offer previously made to him by

Chard to stay and help the defence.*

Dalton's plan for the defence of the mission station made use of all the scanty natural advantages of the position. The rear, or southern front was based on the two buildings. The store house was eighty feet long and twenty deep. It had solid stone walls, twelve feet high. There were no windows at the back and the door at the eastern end was solidly barricaded. Forty yards to the west of the store, which Witt had used as a chapel, was the Witts' home, now the hospital. It was not so substantially built as the store and was a honeycomb of small rooms, several of which opened only to the rear and western end of the building, the open flank.

As soon as it was decided that the hospital must form part of the perimeter, Reynolds, with his orderlies and eight or ten convalescent patients, started to loophole the outer walls. There was no time to move the bed-ridden patients. As soon as the main line of the rest of the defence was laid out, Bromhead allocated a handful of his men to the defence of the hospital. 'Half a dozen of us were stationed in the hospital with orders to hold it and guard the sick. The ends of the building were built of stone, the side walls of ordinary bricks, and the inside walls, or partitions, of sunburnt bricks of mud. It was a queer little one-storied building, which it is almost impossible to describe; but we were pinned like rats in a hole, because all the doorways but one had been barricaded by mealie bags, and we had done the same with the windows. The patients' beds were simple rough affairs of wood raised only about half a foot above the floor. To talk of 'hospital' or 'ward' conveys the idea of a big building: but as a matter of fact this hospital was a mere little shed or bungalow, divided up into rooms so small that you could hardly swing a bayonet in them.'

The space between the two buildings was filled with two

* Chard did not notice Adendorff's defection and reported that 'he stayed to assist in the defence'. Nevertheless the evidence is overwhelming that he decamped. He was later arrested in Pietermaritzburg. There is also a strong suggestion that he left Isandhlwana earlier than was necessary as he rode by a route which the Zulus cut quite early in the day. He met Sergeant Vane only on the bank of the Buffalo.

wagons, each eighteen feet long. They were still on their wheels but with biscuit and meat boxes filling the gaps underneath the body. Mealie bags were packed on top and with the gaps between the wagons and buildings blocked with boxes and bags, it made an excellent barricade at a convenient height for firing. The field of fire on this north front was good although behind the store there was a shed which had been used as a cook house and, running almost parallel with the rampart and less than twenty yards away, was a two-foot bank with a two-foot ditch on the near side.

The situation was less satisfactory on the northern face. From the western end of the hospital to a point opposite the eastern end of the store was a line of more than ninety yards. Fortunately there was a rocky ledge, or step, two feet high running along the line from a point a few yards in front of the hospital. Along the top of this step a four foot barricade of mealie bags was raised, giving a good aiming rest, sound protection to the defenders' bodies and a six foot obstacle to assailants. Although it was a hot day the men worked with concentrated energy, knowing that their lives depended on their efforts. They succeeded in building the basic perimeter in little more than an hour. As a non-combatant survivor wrote, 'The men worked with a will and were much encouraged by the unremitting exertions of both the military officers, the medical officer and the Assistant Commissary, all of whom not merely directed but joined energetically in the construction of the barricades.'

At its eastern end the long barricade in front of the buildings joined a stone-built cattle-kraal or pound which stood close by the store house, the small gap between the two stone structures being blocked with mealie bags. The kraal itself was divided by a low stone partition. Reluctantly Chard decided to include it in his defences. It was a necessary embarrassment. The walls were solid enough but they were not high enough to give complete body cover to the defenders. Nor since they were too narrow, could mealie bags be placed on them to give extra height. On the other hand, its bullet-proof walls would give too much cover to attackers

91

at a point dangerously close to the heart of the defence. It had to be given a garrison.

The whole circuit of the defences, including the kraal, was nearly four hundred yards. By scraping together every man of B Company and every convalescent who could stand and fire a rifle, there were little more than a hundred trained soldiers to hold the perimeter. There were also the hundred Kaffirs of the NNC who had between them about thirty rifles, most of them old muzzle-loaders. If the field of fire all round the defences had been clear, Chard could reasonably have felt confident for he would be able to use his main, almost his only asset, the fire power of the Martini-Henry rifles. As things stood, there were too many places where the Zulus could get too close to the defenders for their safety. The ditch behind the hospital has already been mentioned. Another hazard was a free-standing cattle kraal, roughly built of stone, which stood only a few yards from the stronger kraal which it had been decided to hold. The rough kraal would be useless to the defence but its walls were bullet-proof and it offered valuable cover in which to form up an assault.

The weakest part of the defence, however, was the western end of the hospital where bushes and trees came right up to the rocky ledge. As if this was not dangerous enough, there was a stone wall, five foot high, less than thirty feet from the mealie bag rampart.

Even behind the ramparts many of the defenders would not be able to feel safe. The ground behind the houses was open but, about two hundred yards away, it started to rise to a series of terraces to the heights of the Oscarberg. From the first of these terraces, which had plenty of covered positions, a marksman would have his sights on the backs of the men holding the front barricade except where the two houses blocked his view. The range would be about three hundred yards. Half a dozen skilled riflemen, if they had the proper ammunition for their weapons, could make the rampart untenable in quarter of an hour.

Chard left no record of his estimate of the garrison's

chances before the attack began. He was probably too busy for abstract calculations. Either the defence held or they would all be massacred. Surgeon-Major Reynolds did weigh the odds. He remembered that 'we did not consider either building would be taken without the fall of the whole', and that the feeling among the officers was that 'comparing our prospects with that of the Isandhlwana affair, we felt that the mealie barriers might afford us a moderately fair chance.'

Having seen the work well under way Chard remounted his horse and galloped back to the drift. The ponts being safely moored, he 'brought up, along with their guard, one sergeant and six men, the gear, wagons etc. I desire to mention for approval the offer of these pont guards, Daniels [the civilian ferryman] and Sergeant Milne of the 3rd Buffs, who with their comrades, volunteered to moor the ponts out in the middle of the stream, and there to defend them from the decks, with a few men to assist.' He refused this gallant offer. Eight extra men with rifles behind the rampart would be of more value than the dubious advantage of defending a single river crossing. Moreover, if the Zulus were to concern themselves with the drift, Milne and his party could only delay them for a short time at the inevitable cost of their deaths. It would be impossible to keep up their supply of ammunition and, exposed on the open decking of the ponts, they would be certain targets for even the incompetent Zulu marksmen. Bringing the water cart, they marched up to the mission.

Chard returned to the fortification at about 3.30 pm.* There he found two very frightened men. Otto Witt, the missionary, and George Smith, the chaplain, had stayed with a single soldier on top of the Oscarberg in blissful ignorance of their danger. They saw flames rising from a farm on the Natal side of the river near Fugitives' Drift 'but

* As in all battles, exact timings are hard to establish. Chard gives this time as 3.30. Surgeon Major Reynolds, a most reliable witness, gives 3.30 as the time of the start of the Zulu attack but he seems to have been about an hour and a half out.

we were so far from fancying that the Zulus would cross the river that we never had the slightest idea of the real state of things'. 5,000 Zulus were moving towards them but 'we were still thinking that the approaching black men were our own troops. They got so close to us that their bullets could easily have reached us, and we saw that they were all naked. Reality, then, stood naked before us. Those who had crossed the river and were approaching were Zulus. We speedily descended the hill.'

Witt lost no time in galloping away from the mission. He told anyone who had the time to listen that he was concerned for his family whom he believed to be at Umsinga, twenty miles away. Eventually he was re-united with them in Durban where, according to a Natal paper, he was convicted for pointing a loaded gun at a Kaffir woman who refused to do the family washing. He soon sailed for England where he enjoyed a brief blaze of glory by claiming to be a survivor of both Isandhlwana and Rorke's Drift. George Smith, meanwhile, was anxiously searching for his horse. Finding that his Kaffir groom had stolen it to make his own escape, the chaplain stayed to help the defenders and became a hero despite himself.

Throughout the afternoon stragglers from Isandhlwana, some singly, some in small groups, came to the mission. They were colonial volunteers from the Natal Carbineers and the Mounted Police. They all rode on to Helpmakaar. It is impossible to blame them. They were exhausted and in a state of shock. Regular soldiers might have been expected to have stood and fought it out but the volunteers, brave as most of them were, were not under the tight, all-embracing discipline of professionals. Only one possible reinforcement reported to Chard. This was a troop of Sikhali's Horse, a hundred strong under Lieutenant Vause, which rode up from Fugitives' Drift. They had seen little of the battle at Isandhlwana as they had been guarding Durnford's baggage and had only approached the camp as the defence disintegrated. They had not seen the full horror of the holocaust, as had the other fugitives, and were still a formed body under their own officer.

This was a most heartening accession of strength. They could act as an early warning screen which was badly needed. Reports were coming in, mostly from terrified stragglers, of vast Zulu hordes descending on the mission from all points of the compass. Lack of information always breeds chimeras and it was impossible to send out dismounted patrols. No British infantryman could hope to outrun a Zulu party. The only effective look-out was Private Frederick Hitch sitting astride the apex of the hospital roof. Moreover when the attack came in, the men of Sikhali's Horse would be valuable, as they were all armed with Martini-Henry rifles. They would bring the defensive strength of the post up to one modern rifle to every six feet of the perimeter.

When Vause asked Chard for orders, 'I requested him to send a detachment to observe the drift and ponts and to throw out vedettes in the direction of the enemy in order to check their advance as much as possible, his men falling back upon the post when forced to retire, and thereafter to assist the defence.'

The horsemen trotted off to take up their positions in a great arc which ran from the drift to the north, round the east and south of the mission and finishing with a vedette on the summit of the Oscarberg. Chard then called a halt to the building work. The wall was at least four feet high all round the perimeter and further toil would only exhaust the men who had already done almost two hours of heaving the heavy mealie bags and boxes. Panting men do not aim well and he was anxious that they should have time to get their breath back before the attack came. With Bromhead, he moved slowly round the walls, placing each man in his firing position, allocating areas of responsibility to sergeants and corporals, interspersing the stolid, reliable Welshmen of the Twenty-Fourth* with the unknown quantities of colonial

* Although the Twenty-Fourth were designated the 2nd Warwickshires, they were almost entirely recruited in Wales and had had their depot in Brecon since 1873. They were renamed South Wales Borderers in 1881.

troopers and such of the NNC as had modern rifles. Water-bottles were filled from the cart. Ammunition boxes were opened. Pouches were filled and beside every man was laid out a small pile of rounds for immediate use. When every man was in his place, Bromhead gave the order to fix bayonets and all round the ramparts there was a 'click, click' as the twenty-four-inch triangular bayonets were fitted to the muzzles. Every precaution had been taken.

At 4.20 there was a spattering of musketry from behind the Oscarberg. Lieutenant Vause galloped back to the barricade, 'reporting that the enemy was now close to us. His men, he told me [Chard], would not obey orders, but were going off towards Helpmakaar, and I myself saw them in retreat, numbering apparently 100, going in that direction.' Vause dug in his spurs and followed them as fast as his horse could go. He may have tried to rally them.

At a stroke the firepower of the garrison had been cut almost in half. Worse than that, a hundred well-armed horsemen had defected in full view of the garrison. Even the bravest man must have felt his heart sink. The effect on the Natal Native Contingent was decisive. To a man they heaved themselves over the walls and legged it away to the south. Captain Stephenson went with them. Infuriated, some of the Twenty-Fourth fired into their rapidly retreating backs before the officers could restrain them. They brought down one European. Another sergeant, Duncan Moody, stayed behind and fought through the battle.

The defence was now down to one hundred rifles, one to every twelve feet of the perimeter. This was obviously not enough. The hospital had been included especially so that there should be space within the walls for the N.N.C. Now they were gone, the garrison could not hope to hold out indefinitely. If the Zulus were to launch a concerted attack from all sides at the same time they must break through. 'I saw,' wrote Chard, 'that our line of defence was too extended for the small number of men now left, and at once commenced an inner retrenchment of biscuit boxes.'

Chard's new rampart was a wall seventy foot long projecting from the western wall of the store house to the point where it met the front barricade. The little fortress it made had a perimeter of little more than a hundred yards including the stone kraal. In a desperate situation the latter could be evacuated bringing the circuit of the defence down to seventy yards of which one third consisted of the solid twelve foot walls of the store house. Material was put ready to block the entrance to the kraal if it became necessary and, in the centre of the inner fortress, a mound of mealie bags, nine feet high, began to be built. From the top of this riflemen would be able to fire over the heads of those manning the rampart.

The garrison would be safe as soon as these final preparations were complete. A hundred men with rifles and a plentiful supply of ammunition, firing from behind an adequate fortification could not be defeated by an enemy without artillery unless there was a general collapse of morale. Whatever secret fears Chard may have entertained, he can scarcely have contemplated that B Company, 2nd battalion, Twenty-Fourth Foot would panic. The British infantryman is not without his faults but the dogged defence of a position had always been his *forte*. As General Reille told Napoleon on the morning of Waterloo, 'British infantry in position are impregnable because of their quiet steadiness and their excellent fire discipline.' Napoleon had not believed him but Napoleon had been wrong. Sixty-four years later the quiet steadiness of the British infantry was still a rock on which a commander could build, whatever else was dangerous and uncertain.

Chard's problem was whether his new inner retrenchment would be ready in time. A seventy foot wall had to be built out of biscuit boxes, each weighing a hundredweight, by men who had already performed herculean feats of construction under a blazing sun. When that was done, the patients must be moved from the hospital to the dubious shelter of the store house verandah. The decision to delay their evacuation was a hard one. The safety of all, fit or sick, depended on the new wall being made high enough to form a safe defence.

97

Until that was done every man who could be spared from guard duty must be used to heave the biscuit boxes.

It was impossible to tell how soon the attack might come. All the information was that somewhere behind the Oscarberg was a large body of Zulus. There could be other bodies in other directions. The main Zulu army, intoxicated by its triumph at Isandhlwana, might be pouring down the road to Rorke's Drift. For information Chard depended on Private Hitch on the hospital roof. Hitch could see no one. The attack might start in five minutes or five hours.

It was right to leave the patients where they were until the inner ring was complete but, inevitably, it caused trouble later. The retreat into the last redoubt had to be delayed while the sick were moved in the middle of the attack but if they had been moved earlier there might have been no inner ring to defend. If anyone made an error of judgment at this stage it was Surgeon-Major Reynolds. It seems possible that he, with the three other ranks of the Army Hospital Corps, could have moved the twelve patients who were in the rooms with doors which opened only outside the perimeter. There are a dozen possible reasons why this was not done and, from what is known of Reynolds, it can be assumed that his reasons were valid at the time.

About five o'clock,* the final box was pushed into place. The new wall was four feet high. There was a shout from the hospital roof as Private Hitch slid down the thatch to the ground. 'Here they come! Black as hell and thick as grass!'

---

* Once more the time is difficult to establish with certainty. Both Chard and the chaplain say that the attack started at 4.30 but Chard also says that it was at 4.20 that Vause reported that his horsemen were decamping. Still, according to Chard, it was after this that the NNC left and only subsequently was the inner retrenchment started. Up to this point all Chard's timings seem to be true but it seems impossible that the seventy foot wall could have been completed before five o'clock. Certainly Chard had more than enough on his mind at this moment to check with his watch and it seems probable that the chaplain took the time from Chard's despatch, which was published soon after the battle.

CHAPTER 8

Onslaught

There were three Zulu regiments behind the Oscarberg. Two of them were composed of married men, wearing the head-ring. These were the uThulwana, whose warriors were 45 years old, and the uDloko, who were 41-year-olds. With them was the 33-year-old, unmarried, inDlu-yengwe regiment. Although it is always hard to give an accurate estimate of Zulu numbers, it seems certain that the whole force was 4,000 strong and may have been as many as 4,500.

All three regiments had formed part of the right 'horn' at Isandhlwana which had come round to the west of the great hill. They had all been on the outside of the arc and such fighting as that 'horn' had done had been the work of the inner regiments, the uNokenke, umKhulutshane, the uDududu and the isiNgqu. The two older regiments had done nothing more spectacular than block the track to Rorke's Drift while the younger inDlu-yengwe had continued their advance to Fugitives' Drift. They had inflicted many casualties on the fugitives but, for some reason which has never been explained, they did not block the road to the drift which was the only escape route open to the survivors. A few detachments had crossed the Buffalo and murdered a few wounded or exhausted men, probably including Melvill and Coghill with the Queen's Colour of the Twenty-Fourth. Some kind of rearguard had been improvized on the Natal bank of the river and the fragments of the inDlu-yengwe which did ford the river soon recrossed, having suffered a few casualties.

They did not feel that they had distinguished themselves

99

in battle. They had not come up against any formed body of their enemy and, while the rest of the army had won a great victory, the inDlu-yengwe were concerned that it might be said that they had not washed their spears. They were tired from a trotting march of more than ten miles, short of food and lacking positive leadership since their commander, Usibebu had been one of their few casualties and his deputy had not had time to assert his authority.

For a time they wandered aimlessly upstream. Seeing some farm buildings on the Natal bank, some warriors crossed again and set fire to them. The remainder drifted across and it was on the south bank that they were formed up again. As a formed body they continued to move upstream but, as far as can be seen, they had no particular object in view except, perhaps, some more fire-raising and, if opportunity offered, some looting.

A mile or more up the river a dry watercourse comes into the Buffalo from the north. In its bed they caught sight of the uThulwana and the uDloko, who had been combing the country for survivors from the camp and, having reached the river, had settled down to rest. In command of them was Dabulamanzi, Cetshwayo's thirty-five-year-old brother. This was the first time he had held an independent command and, like the inDlu-yengwe, he was anxious to distinguish himself. Urged on by the young regiment, he decided to attack the depot of stores which was known to be in the Oscarberg mission.

In undertaking this movement Dabulamanzi was disobeying his royal brother's orders on two counts. Cetshwayo had prohibited any invasion of Natal. If the Zulus were to attack the colony they would need all their available troops to succeed. With three British columns aiming for Ulundi, every warrior was needed for the defence of the homeland. No good would be achieved by making buccaneering raids which could only burn a few buildings and murder some civilians. To do so would alienate the sympathisers Cetshwayo knew he had in Natal and, even more, in Britain. This prohibition was not evidence of the king's pacifism but of his sound

100

7. A preliminary sketch for the painting 'The Defence of Rorke's Drift', by Lady Elizabeth Butler (see front of jacket). Lady Butler arranged for members of the 24th Regiment to pose for her on their return to England, and this and the following three illustrations clearly exhibit the way in which she built up the composition of the final painting

8. A rough drawing showing an early version of the overall design

9. A private of the Twenty-Fourth aiming his Martini-Henry

10. This figure bears a close resemblance to the soldier leaning over the mealie bags on the left of the finished picture

11. The men who held Rorke's Drift: the survivors photographed on 22 January, 1879

12. The commissariat store stripped of its thatch after the action. The slopes of the Oscarberg heights can also be seen

military and political sense.

He had also forbidden attacks on fortified places. This again was good military sense. In the open field massed manpower armed with the assegai had a reasonable chance of defeating small bodies of men with single-loading rifles, especially if they were interspersed with unreliable elements who started the campaign in mortal fear of the Zulus. Against fortifications with an adequate garrison the odds would be heavily against the assegai. There were no flanks to turn, no open rear. At Isandhlwana the impis had made no headway in frontal attacks against steady infantry. The disaster occurred because the Twenty-Fourth were deployed with their flanks in the air. When Dabulamanzi disobeyed this order he could, of course, plead that he did not know that, with great skill and enormous exertion, the mission had been turned into a fortress.

Having decided on the attack, Dabulamanzi felt that he must employ his whole available strength. Since he was disobeying orders, the only excuse could be unqualified victory. He ordered the two older regiments to join the inDlu-yengwe on the south bank. It was a dangerous and difficult operation. The stream was wide, deep and running fast. Several of those who first tried to cross were swept away and battered on the rocks downstream. It was only when chains of men, arms linked, shuffled across from either bank and joined in the middle of the river that it was possible for the 3,000 men of the uThulwana and the uDloko to start edging their way across. Once all were on the Natal side they rested and took snuff. Then they moved slowly to the eastern foot of the Oscarberg where their appearance gave such a shock to the two reverend gentlemen on the summit.

Dabulamanzi's determination to use all his regiments in a single smashing blow cost him his best chance of success. Had he sent the inDlu-yengwe straight to the mission at their best pace they would have arrived before even the original perimeter was complete. Being at least a thousand strong, they could hardly have failed to overrun the garrison which then included a hundred nervous Kaffirs. The two older regiments could have made their way upstream on the northern bank to cross at the undefended and indefensible Rorke's Drift in no more time than it would have taken them to reach the mission by crossing with great difficulty where they did.

They received a few wild shots from Vause's horsemen which may have checked their approach march slightly and they made their first attack from the south at five o'clock. Chard reported, 'Five hundred or six hundred of the enemy came suddenly in sight around the hill to the south [the Oscarberg]. They advanced at a run against our south wall but were met with a well-sustained fire; yet, notwithstanding heavy loss, they continued to advance to within fifty yards of the wall, when their leading men encountered such a hot fire from our front with a cross one from the store, that they were checked.'

This first assault was doomed to failure. The south wall, buttressed by two wagons, was the most secure part of the whole perimeter. As yet the Zulus had no idea how formidable the opposition was in numbers or in fortification. Normally the Zulus were very meticulous in reconnaissance since their encircling technique could only succeed if the enemy's position and weak points were pin-pointed in advance. At Isandhlwana, Zulu scouts had been seen in many directions for several hours before the attack developed. It seems that Dabulamanzi had neglected to take the elementary precaution of having a careful look at his objective from the top of the Oscarberg. It is unlikely that the anxious watchers in the mission would have failed to see him had he, or any other Zulus, done so. Such neglect suggests that he assumed his self-appointed task was an easy one.

The survivors of the first rush sought what cover they could around the cookhouse shack and its detached oven or in the drainage ditch and the bank behind the hospital. Many of the warriors had firearms of a sort as well as their assegais and they opened a heavy if not a damaging fire. Behind them a huge column of Zulus swung wide round the hospital and formed, under cover of the bushes, for an attack on the north west corner of the defences.

When they were ready they advanced 'in skirmishing order at a slow slinging run. We opened fire on them from the hospital at 600 yards and, although the bullets ploughed through their midst and knocked many over, there was no check or alteration made in their approach. They seemed quite regardless of the danger, and what struck me as most strange they had no war cry, nor did they at this time fire a single shot in return.'

One of the defenders of the hospital was Private Henry Hook, who was cookhouse orderly that day. He remembered how the Zulus 'took advantage of every bit of cover there was—anthills, a tract of bush we had not time to clear away, a garden or sort of orchard which was near us. They neglected nothing and large bodies kept hurling themselves against our slender breastworks. It was the hospital they assaulted most fiercely. I had charge, with a man we called "Old King Cole", of a small room* with only one patient in it. Cole kept with me for some time after the fight began, then he said he was not going to stay. He went outside and was instantly killed by the Zulus; so that I was left alone with the patient—a native whose leg was broken, and who kept crying out: "Take my bandage off, so that I can come!" But it was impossible to do anything except fight and I blazed away as fast as I could. Poor "Old King Cole" was lying dead outside, and the helpless patient was crying and groaning near me. The Zulus were swarming around us, and there was an extraordinary rattle as the bullets struck the biscuit-boxes and queer thuds as they plumped into the bags of mealies. Then there was the whizz and rip of the assegais. We had plenty of ammunition but we were told to save it, and so we took careful aim with every shot and hardly a cartridge was wasted. I was a marksman in my company and I dropped some of them. One of them, sheltering behind an anthill, I had three shots at. I remember that I went out the

* This was the room at the extreme south-western corner of the building. It had an outside door and another which connected with the inside of the building.

103

next day to see whether I'd hit him the third time. He was lying behind the ant hill with a hole in his skull. One of my comrades, Private Dunbar, shot no fewer than nine Zulus, one of them being a chief.'

In charge of the section of wall in front of the hospital was Commissary Dalton. Chaplain Smith was full of admiration for him. 'He is a very tall man and was continually going along the barricade, fearlessly exposing himself, cheering the men and using his own rifle most effectively. A Zulu ran up near the barricade; Mr Dalton called out—"Pot that fellow" and himself aimed over the parapet at another, when his rifle dropped, he turned quite pale and said he had been shot. The doctor was by his side at once, and found that a bullet had passed quite through, above the right shoulder. Unable to use his rifle (although he did not cease to direct the fire of the men who were near him), he handed it to Mr Byrne [an Assistant Store Keeper in the Commissariat Department], who used it well. Presently Corporal Scammel, Natal Native Contingent [a hospital patient], who was near Mr Byrne, was shot through the shoulder and back. He crawled a short distance and handed the remainder of his cartridges to Lieutenant Chard and then expressed his desire for a drink of water; Byrne at once fetched him one, and whilst giving it to him to drink poor Byrne was shot through the head and fell dead instantly.'

Dalton, Scammel and Byrne had all been shot in the back by Zulus with rifles firing from caves and from behind rocks on the terraces of the Oscarberg. At a range of as little as three or four hundred yards these riflemen could look down onto the backs of the soldiers defending the front wall of the perimeter. Fortunately for the garrison, the remarkable military virtues of the Zulus did not include marksmanship. Nor did they receive much assistance from their weapons. Most of the rifles were muzzle-loading flintlocks, mass-produced and frequently substandard. They were made as cheaply as possibly in Birmingham for an eager market among primitive peoples who stood in superstitious awe of firearms, regarding them as much as a status symbol as a weapon. They were not the kind of product which a gun-smith would go to the trouble and expense of sending to the Proof House. In consequence, it was unwise to load them with a full charge of powder lest the barrel explode in the firer's face. Powder, in any case, was always in short supply and properly fashioned musket balls, giving a close fit in the barrel, were almost unprocurable. The usual missile was a roughly hammered metal 'slug' which would be eccentric in flight but gave an ugly jagged wound if it happened to hit somebody.

A few of the Zulus had more modern weapons. For the most part these were Sniders, the rifle which the British regulars had discarded five years earlier and which colonial formations, such as the NNC still carried. It was a breech-loader which had been designed to be fired by percussion caps but which had later been converted to fixed ammuni-tion, that is, rounds which are self-contained with a bullet, charge of powder and detonator. This was a great dis-advantage from the Zulu point of view since, unlike flintlock ammunition, it could not be home-made. Some was imported into Zululand from Portuguese East Africa, some was smuggled in from Natal but there was never enough to main-tain the kind of continuous fusilade which would have made Chard's barricades untenable. Nevertheless the Snider, which was sighted up to 950 yards, packed a heavy punch. The bullet had a calibre of 0.577", almost twice the size of bullets of World War II, and the wounds it inflicted were corres-pondingly severe.

To keep down this dropping fire from the terraces, Chard and Bromhead posted a handful of marksmen along the south wall between the two buildings. Since only their helmets were exposed to the men on the terraces, these defenders were reasonably safe from the inaccurate fire from the Oscarberg. They were experienced experts and had a weapon which gave them plenty of scope. The Martini-Henry was the best service rifle of its day, its only serious drawback being that it was a single shot weapon. To load it the breech block had to be lowered by pulling down a lever behind the trigger guard. This uncovered the breech and ejected the spent cartridge case. At 'rapid fire' twelve aimed rounds a minute could be fired and the bullet was .45", less than the Snider but certainly a man-stopper even if the target was a charging Zulu. Its most effective range was four hundred yards but it was sighted up to 1,450.* According to Sir Garnet Wolseley, 'it shoots well up to over 3,000 yards'! From the firer's point of view the main disadvantage of the Martini was its kick. Continuous firing was certain to bruise the shoulder and if it was loosed off carelessly, before it was held in firmly to the shoulder, it could break the collar bone.

The targets on the terraces of the Oscarberg were well-concealed and revealed themselves only by the muzzle flash which was immediately obscured by a large puff of black smoke. Both sides were using black powder and each time a round was fired the marksman obscured his own vision. If there was any wind he also blinded temporarily his comrade to leeward. If there was no wind the smoke would hang about in clouds and after an hour or two of heavy firing could make accurate shooting very difficult.

At the front rampart the defenders had troubles enough without a shower of shots from behind them. The Zulus charged repeatedly and were met with rapid fire. Their losses would have discouraged men less brave and less determined but many of the warriors pressed on and crossed their stabbing assegais with the twenty-four inch triangular bayonets of the Twenty-Fourth as they tried to scramble over the mealie bags. To return to the chaplain's account, 'The garden and the road—having a stone wall and thick belt of

* It is interesting to compare the Martini-Henry with its World War II equivalent:

Weight	Length of Barrel	Calibre	Max. rate of aimed fire	Penetration of sandbags at 40 yds
Martini-Henry Mk II (1876)				
9 lb 2 oz	33¼ ins	0.450 ins	12 rpm	12 ins
S.M.L.E. Mk VI (1940)				
9 lb 1 oz	25.2 ins	0.303 ins	25 rpm	17 ins

bushes as a screen from our front defence—were now occupied by a large force of the enemy. They rushed up to the front barricade and soon occupied one side while we held the other. They seized hold of the bayonets of our men and in two instances succeeded in wresting them off the rifles, but the bold perpetrators were instantly shot. One fellow fired at Corporal Schiess, of the Natal Native Contingent (a Swiss by birth who was a hospital patient), blowing his hat off: he instantly jumped on the parapet and bayonetted the man, regained his place and shot another and then, repeating his former exploit, climbed on the parapet and bayonetted a third. A bullet struck him on the instep early in the fight but he would not allow that his wound was a sufficient reason for leaving his post.'

The Zulu pressure was so great that Chard had been forced to postpone the evacuation of the hospital although he knew it to be essential. He was having to defend an area larger than his garrison could cover adequately and if he withdrew men from the walls, the Zulus might make a breakthrough. The question was decided by the enemy. Soon after six o'clock a throwing assegai with a tuft of flaming grass was flung onto the thatched roof of the hospital. As the garrison saw this there was a slackening of their fire and the Zulus, taking advantage of the lull, managed to secure a lodgement inside the north-west corner of the barricade. 'Some of them' wrote the Surgeon-Major, 'gained the hospital verandah and there got hand-to-hand with our men defending the doors. Once they were driven back from here to find shelter again in the garden, but others soon pressed forward in their stead and occupied the verandah in larger numbers.'

Gonville Bromhead surmounted this crisis. Gathering a few men together he charged time and again from the inner rampart to the front of the hospital, each time clearing the Zulus back to the outer defences. He could not hope to hold them back for long. Their numbers must eventually force him back behind the inner wall. His task was to buy time while the patients were evacuated.

The evacuation had to be carried out by the handful of men who formed the garrison, no one else could be spared to help them. To make matters worse the only door to the building which opened within the defences was on the verandah and could not be used, as it was in the centre of Bromhead's fight.

Henry Hook described how the garrison of the hospital reacted to the firing of the thatched roof. 'This put us in a terrible plight, because it meant that we were either to be massacred or burnt alive or get out of the building. To get out seemed impossible for, if we left the hospital by the only door which had been left open, the others having been blocked up, we should instantly fall into the midst of the Zulus. Besides, there were the helpless sick and wounded and we could not leave them. My own little room communicated with another by means of a frail little door like a bedroom door. Fire and dense choking smoke forced me to get out of my own room and go into another. It was impossible for me to take the native patient with me,* and I had to leave him to an awful fate. But his death was, at any rate, a merciful one. I heard the Zulus asking him questions, and he tried to tear his bandages off and escape.

'In the room where I was now there were nine sick men, and I was alone to look after them for some time, still firing away with the hospital burning. Suddenly in the thick smoke I saw John Williams, who had rushed in through a doorway communicating with another room and above the din of battle and the cries of the wounded, I heard him shout, "The Zulus are all over the place! They've dragged Joseph Williams out and killed him!"

'John Williams had held the adjoining room with Private Harrigan† for more than an hour until they had not a cartridge left. The Zulus had then burst in and dragged out Joseph Williams and two of the patients and assegaied them.

---

* The 'native patient' with a broken thigh was a prisoner of war, captured in the attack on Sihayo's kraal on 12 January. Hook may have hoped that it would be safe to leave him to his compatriots.

† A hospital patient of 1st battalion, Twenty-Fourth.

It was only because they were so busy with this slaughtering that John Williams and two of the patients were able to knock a hole in the partition and get into the room where I was posted. Harrigan was killed.

'What were we to do? We were pinned like rats in a hole. Already the Zulus were fiercely trying to burst in through the doorway. The only way of escape was the wall itself—by making a hole big enough for a man to crawl through into an adjoining room, and so on until we got outside. Williams worked desperately at the wall with the navvy's pick which I had been using to make some of the loopholes with.

'All this time the Zulus were trying to get into the room. Their assegais kept whizzing towards us, and one struck me in front of the helmet. We were wearing the white tropical helmets then. But the helmet tilted back under the blow and made the spear lose its power, so that I escaped with a scalp wound, which did not trouble me much then.

'Only one man at a time could get in at the door. A big Zulu sprang forward and seized my rifle; but I tore it free and, slipping a cartridge in, I shot him point-blank. Time after time the Zulus gripped the muzzle and tried to tear the rifle from me, and time after time I wrenched it back, because I had a better grip than they had.

'All this time Williams was getting the sick through the hole into the next room—all except one, a soldier of the Twenty-Fourth named Connolly, who could not move because of a broken leg. Watching for my chance I dashed from my doorway, and grabbing Connolly, I pulled him after me through the hole. His leg got broken again but there was no help for it. As soon as we left the room the Zulus burst in with furious cries of disappointment and rage.

'Now there was a repetition of the work of holding the doorway, except I had to stand by a hole in the wall instead of a door while Williams picked away at the far wall to make an opening to escape into the next room. There was more desperate and almost hopeless fighting, as it seemed, but most of the poor fellows were got through the hole.

Again I had to drag Connolly through, a terrific task because he was a heavy man.

'Privates William Jones and Robert Jones* during all this time had been doing magnificent work in another ward which faced the hill. They kept at it with bullet and bayonet until six of the seven patients in that ward had been removed. They would have got the seventh—Sergeant Maxfield—out safely but he was delirious with fever and, although they managed to dress him, he refused to move. Robert Jones made a last rush to try and get him away like the rest; but when he got back into the room he saw that Maxfield was being stabbed by the Zulus as he lay on his bed.

'We—Williams, and R. Jones and W. Jones and myself—were the last men to leave the hospital after most of the sick and wounded had been carried through a small window and away from the burning, but it was impossible to save a few of them and they were butchered.'

Leaving the hospital was an agonizing business for the patients. The window through which they had to be squeezed was six foot above ground level. The only help they had was from Private Hitch, the former look-out and he had only one usable arm, the other had been disabled by a Zulu 'slug'. It is hard to imagine the pain suffered by Connolly with his newly re-broken leg, either as he hit the hard-packed earth of the courtyard or when, a few minutes later, Henry Hook picked him up and carried him on his back to the inner retrenchment.

Trooper Hunter of the Natal Mounted Police was even more unfortunate. He had rheumatism in his legs so badly that he could not walk. Having reached the ground he tried

---

* As in all Welsh regiments there is a confusing shortage of surnames. For the sake of clarity the following is the nominal role of the defenders of the hospital:

   801   Private Cole, Thomas. *Killed in Action.*
 1373   Private Hook, Henry.
  716   Private Jones, Robert.
  593   Private Jones, William.
 1393   Private Williams, John.
 1398   Private Williams, Joseph. *Killed in Action.*

to inch his way to the biscuit box barricade with his elbows. By this time Bromhead's desperate charges had been finally driven back and the courtyard was kept clear of Zulus only by volley firing, directed by Chard at the inner barricade. Hunter was struck and killed by an assegai as he crawled towards safety.

The luckiest man was Gunner Arthur Howard. He was a fever patient, dazed but mobile. Instead of going out through the window he made a dash for the verandah. As he emerged he miraculously escaped both Zulu assegais and Chard's volleys. In utter confusion he failed to turn right towards his comrades but dashed straight ahead and vaulted the front wall of mealie bags. Realizing his mistake he dashed to a small bush, collapsed and feigned dead, pulling long grass over himself. 'He was equally exposed to the Zulu assegais and the English bullets. His greatest anxiety was to cover the red stripe of his overalls which seemed to him to show very clearly in the darkness. He was nearly discovered several times—once by a stray pig, who had been struck down close to him by a stray bullet, and whose acclamations attracted attention.' Several times the gunner was trodden on by Zulus but he lay still all through the night and was able, at dawn, to return to the barricades.

For the garrison, the situation was much more secure once the evacuation of the hospital was complete. Since the stone-built storehouse covered their backs, they were no longer exposed to sniping from the Oscarberg. Their hastily built ramparts were showing themselves proof against all the weapons of the enemy although one man was unlucky enough to be wounded in the neck by a 'slug' which found its way through a small gap between two biscuit boxes. The most exposed part of the perimeter was now the stone kraal at the right front of the line. It was no longer serving an essential purpose and put men at risk unnecessarily. Chard decided to evacuate it but before ordering the move, he set about constructing yet another interior fortress. He had been much impressed by the ability of the Zulus to scale defended ramparts, he resolved that there must everywhere

111

be a second line of defence.

With the help of Assistant Commissary Dunne and a few men, he started work on the heap of mealie bags, already nine feet high and cone-shaped, which had been built to enable men to fire over the heads of those manning the ramparts. The top of the cone was removed and a number of sacks removed from the heart of those which remained. The truncated stack formed, according to the Surgeon-Major, 'a sheltered space sufficient to accommodate about forty men* and in a position to make good shooting.'

This edible fortress stood hard against the stone wall which divided the enclosure from the kraal and the latter had to be held while it was being constructed. By enormous exertions it was completed before the sudden African fall of night. Even the difficult business of evacuating the kraal, the defenders falling back first to the low dividing partition and then to the mound of mealie bags, was finished while the light lasted.

Reynolds' surgery was now the verandah of the store house and there he operated under what Hook described as 'heavy fire and clouds of assegais'. Working under these conditions he extracted 'slugs' from wounds, re-set and splinted Connolly's leg, extricated thirty-six pieces of bone from Hitch's shattered scapula and calmly attended to every other wound, great or small. Stretcher-cases were accommodated in the centre of the mealie mound but every man who could use a rifle returned to the ramparts and continued to shoot it out with the enemy. Those, like Hitch, who could not shoot carried ammunition to those who could but the moving spirit of the ammunition supply was that red-bearded giant of the church militant, Chaplain Smith.

Above Reynolds' operating theatre, three or four soldiers lay on the roof of the storehouse. They added their quota to the defensive fire but their most important function was

---

* On Chard's scale plan of the defence this redoubt had exterior measurements of 18 feet by 15. Allowing that the walls were two feet thick, probably an underestimate, it seems unlikely that forty men could have fought in it.

to give warning of impending attacks and to douse the flaming assegais which the Zulus repeatedly flung into the thatch, hoping to fire the storehouse as they had the hospital. Each time one of these lodged in the roof, the men had to abandon their scanty cover behind the ridge, edge their way down the forward slope, their ammunition boots slipping on the dry thatch, seize the assegai and throw it back to the ground, beat out the flames with their hands and climb back over the ridge. All this was carried out under a hail of assegais and 'slugs'.

All the defenders had realized that the coming of darkness would make their task far more difficult. Under its cover the Zulus could creep, undetected, to the foot of the ramparts and pour over in a sudden overwhelming rush. The burning of the hospital roof, a near disaster when it occurred, was now their ally. As night fell the building blazed up, 'lighting the scene for hundreds of yards round'. According to Hook, 'It gave us a splendid light to fight by. I believe that it was this light that saved us. We could see them coming and they could not rush us and take us by surprise at any point.'

Night gave no respite from the Zulu attacks. The garrison had been able to concentrate their strength but the Zulus could do the same. The riflemen on the Oscarberg no longer had targets and they came down to add their numbers to the attackers. Excluding the invulnerable back of the storehouse, the perimeter now measured only sixty-five yards and more than 3,000 Zulus were available to assault it. In fact, the night attacks were concentrated on the northern and eastern ramparts. The warriors were unwilling to charge the biscuit box barricade on the west since they would be silhouetted against the flames of the hospital. It was, perhaps, a sign that they were tiring. Before nightfall there had been no suicidal risk they would not have accepted.

The evening attacks were some of the most determined that were made. Again and again 'they hurled themselves at us. We could sometimes, by the light of the flames, keep them well in sight, so that we could take steady aim and fire coolly. When we could do this they never advanced as far as the barricade, because we shot them down as they ran in on us. But every now and then one or two managed to crawl in and climb over the top of the sacks. They were bayonetted off.'

By this time fatigue was as great an enemy as the Zulus. By 10 o'clock at night every man had been toiling and fighting for eight continuous hours. Shoulders were bruised and raw with the recoil of the rifles. Fingertips of the left hand were burned and blistered from the heat of the barrel. Even the rifles which had served so well were starting to give trouble. 'We did so much firing that they became hot and the brass of the cartridges softened and the cartridge chamber jammed. My own rifle jammed several times and I had to work away with the ramrod till I cleared it.' It was a well-known fault of the Martini-Henry that the rifling of the barrel was cut very deeply and squarely so that they fouled up at an early stage. This increased the recoil and eventually necessitated hard work with the ramrod and a patch of metal gauze. In the last resort the men depended on their bayonets. Most of these stood up to the strain splendidly and, when fixed, enabled the troops to overreach the stabbing assegais. A few were found to have been insufficiently tempered and buckled in use.

It was on Chard that the strain fell most heavily, although he showed no sign of it. With all his men concentrated in the storehouse perimeter he could feel reasonably secure for the time being. The losses among the fit men had hardly been serious. B Company had lost only three killed and three seriously wounded, although many more had light flesh wounds. It was only among the bed-bound patients that heavy losses had occurred. The ammunition supply was still very adequate, but Chard had to think of the future. The Zulus seemed prepared to go on attacking until they finally wore the defence down. There must come a time when human nature, and cartridges, would fail under the demands made on them. By nightfall even the indomitable Surgeon-Major was 'beginning to consider our situation rather hopeless'.

The chances of relief seemed slight. They knew that the camp at Isandhlwana had been wiped out. Chelmsford's force had included a high proportion of native troops and no one at the mission would place any reliance on them. Besides, one of the panic-stricken fugitives who had passed them before the attack had called out as he rode that 'the general's party had been broken up into small lots, each trying to get back into the colony by any route'. This might or might not be true but, as the night wore on, it would be increasingly easy to believe. It was useless to look for help from the rear. Major Spalding had ridden off to bring forward a company from Helpmakaar but a single company would stand no chance fighting its way through open country in the midst of a horde of Zulus. The entire garrison of Helpmakaar consisted of only two companies and if, as seemed certain, the Zulus had followed up their Isandhlwana success by a full-scale invasion of Natal, Helpmakaar would not be able to spare a thought, far less a man, for Rorke's Drift. It would have raised Chard's apprehensions greatly if he had known that during the afternoon Major Spalding had been within three miles of the Oscarberg and had turned back.

The last heavy Zulu attack came in shortly before midnight. By this time the flames from the hospital were dying down but as the mass of black figures, brandishing their assegais and baying their war cry '*Usutu! Usutu!*, dashed up to the walls they were met with the same steady fire as before. Once more the majority fell before they reached the walls. Once more a few managed to scramble over the mealie bags only to be met with rifle butts and the wicked twenty-four inch bayonets which could pin a man to the ground through the chest.

Then, after seven hours of firing, there was comparative silence. There was still some desultory and ineffective firing from the Oscarberg and from the bushes beyond the hospital but there were no targets for the Martinis. Chard and Bromhead had a hurried consultation and decided to stand down

115

every second man. There could be no question of rest. In any case every man was under such nervous strain that sleep would have been impossible. There were many essential tasks to be undertaken. The barricades had to be patched, wounded men moved to safer or more comfortable positions. More ammunition had to be distributed and a few biscuits served out to the men still manning the ramparts.

Water was the greatest need. Every waterbottle was long since dry and the wounded were desperately thirsty. The throats of the fighting men were parched from the smoke of their rifles. Miraculously the water cart which Sergeant Milne had brought up from the drift, still stood undamaged in the space between the two buildings. Zulus still lurked in the ruins of the hospital but covered by fire from the west wall, 'three or four of us jumped over the boxes and ran and fetched some water'.

Once or twice during the night the enemy seemed to be forming for another attack. A menacing rhythmic chant was heard in the shadows. The defenders stood to the parapet, levelled their rifles and waited. Each time nothing happened and, after a pause, they were allowed to stand down.

Dawn came at last, soon after four o'clock. The officers and the sentries peered over the ramparts. There was nothing to be seen except the piles of corpses. Chard set a team to work on the roof of the store house, tearing off the thatch. Weaknesses in the barricades which were shown up by daylight were repaired. After a time small patrols were sent out to seek for the enemy. They moved cautiously, covered by riflemen on the ramparts. They found nothing.

Other men were sent to collect the weapons which lay thick on the ground below the walls. Henry Hook was among the party sent out. 'One of the first things I did was to go up to a man who was still looking over our breastwork with his rifle presented to the spot where so many Zulus had been. I went up to him and said, "Hello! What are you doing here!" He made no answer and did not stir. I went still closer and something in his appearance made me tilt back his helmet. As I did so I saw a bullet mark in his forehead

116

and knew he was dead. I went away and was walking up the bed of a small stream near the drift with my own rifle in my right hand and a bunch of assegais over my left shoulder. I came across an unarmed Zulu lying on the ground. He was apparently dead but bleeding from the leg. Thinking it strange that a dead man should bleed, I hesitated and wondered whether I should go on as other Zulus might be lurking about but I resumed my task. Just as I was passing, the supposed dead man seized the butt of the rifle and tried to drag it away. The bunch of assegais rattled to the ground. Suddenly he released his grasp on the rifle and with the other hand fiercely endeavoured to drag me down. The fight was sharp and short; but it ended by the Zulu being struck in the chest with the butt and knocked to the ground. The rest was over quickly.'

For some of the garrison, the waiting after daylight was almost worse than the battle itself. 'We did not know how soon another attack would be made, but we did know that if the Zulus kept on attacking us it was only a question of time before we were cut to pieces as our comrades a dozen miles away had been destroyed.' To stop the men having time to brood over the future, Chard kept everyone busy. The level of the barricades was raised and the walls of the burned out hospital were dragged down with ropes so that the shell of the building could give no cover to an attacker. The stone of the walls was brought across to the storehouse redoubt to strengthen the wall.

At 7 am Colour Sergeant Bourne gave a great shout of 'Stand To!'. A strong body of Zulus appeared on the hills to the south west. They moved away and, as they disappeared into a valley, a single black figure was seen on the northern side of the post. Half-a-dozen rifles immediately sighted on him but some of the garrison recognized him and he was allowed to come up to the walls. He was a Natal Kaffir who had done odd jobs at the mission. Chard sent him off to Helpmakaar with a hasty note to Major Spalding. As he left, the impi reappeared. It was closer but was moving round the eastern flank. For a time tension mounted but the Zulus

117

kept on at their loping trot and eventually were lost to sight, making for Fugitives' Drift. They were tired, hungry and discouraged.

Eight o'clock came and another body of men was seen on the high ground beyond Rorke's Drift. 'For a long time, and even after red coats were distinguished through our fieldglasses, we believed them to be the enemy, some of them dressed in the kits of those who had fallen at Isandhlwana. Not until the mounted infantry, forming an advanced party, crossed the Buffalo Drift were we convinced of our relief. Then we raised a white flag (for *they* were not certain of us either, seeing the hospital was still smoking) and gave three cheers, really feeling that it was all right for us.'

CHAPTER 9

Encomium

While the defence of Rorke's Drift was in progress, Lord Chelmsford passed the night striding up and down among his sleepless but exhausted men on the fringe of the Isandhlwana battlefield.

The force he had taken out of camp that morning to join Dartnell had achieved nothing. They had marched about eight miles when, at about 10 am, an orderly rode up from the camp with a message from Pulleine saying that there were parties of enemy around Isandhlwana and that it would be unwise to send unladen wagons back to Rorke's Drift. This was in accordance with the orders Chelmsford had given before riding out at dawn and, according to his ADC, 'There was nothing alarming in this report, and the General did not think it necessary to withdraw his force, being satisfied with the arrangements that had been made for the protection of the camp.' As a precaution he sent his naval ADC,* who had the most powerful telescope available, to the top of a nearby hill. He had a clear view of the camp and reported that all was quiet. Chelmsford, therefore, continued his march and set about choosing a site for the column's next camp, about twelve miles from Isandhlwana. Commandant Lonsdale, who had been sick, sought and obtained permission to ride back to camp to arrange for rations for Dartnell's companies of NNC, who had reached the end of their supplies after thirty-six hours away from

* This was Lieutenant Berkeley Milne RN. In 1914, when he was an admiral, he was held responsible, probably unfairly, for the escape to Constantinople of the German warships *Goeben* and *Breslau*.

base.

There was no reason why Chelmsford should have felt any apprehension about the safety of his camp at this time. He had left an adequate force to protect it and he had ordered Durnford's column up to reinforce the garrison. It was not until 1 o'clock that he got a report from an NNC battalion between himself and the camp stating that there was a large Zulu force on the east side of the camp and that the firing of artillery had been heard. On this occasion Chelmsford and all his staff ascended a hill and peered at the camp through their glasses. Bodies of men could be seen moving about but all seemed to be peaceful. Nevertheless, the General decided to ride back to camp with his small mounted escort. The main body of the troops were to stay where they were until further orders.

Hardly had these orders been given when another message came back from the NNC battalion. 'For God's sake, come back with all your men; the camp is surrounded and must be taken unless helped.' The whole of headquarters thought that this message painted the situation in unduly alarmist colours. It seemed impossible that, given common prudence, the camp could be in serious danger. The General did not change his orders but continued to ride back. On the way he was met with the messages sent by Pulleine and Gardner at about 2.30 (see p. 78) saying 'The whole camp is turned out and fighting about a mile to its left flank.'

These reports did not state that the situation was at all serious and Chelmsford seems to have missed the sinister implication that the battle was not being fought in the secure conditions he had imagined but in open country 'about a mile' from the camp. Even if he had grasped what was implied it was by then too late to do anything about it.

Four miles from Isandhlwana they met Commandant Lonsdale, exhausted and dragging his pony behind him. He had ridden to the camp in a fevered daze. The tents were still standing and there were red-coated figures moving about them. He was on the outskirts of the lines when a bullet cracked past his head. Even then it took him some seconds

120

to realize that the redcoats had black faces and that among them were naked warriors with assegais looting the tents and slaughtering the draught cattle. Fortunately they were too absorbed to pay much attention to him and despite the efforts of his starving pony, who remembered where the forage was stacked, he was able to ride away unmolested and bring the news to Chelmsford. The General's reply was, 'But I left 1,000 men to guard the camp.' Immediately he sent an order for the rest of the column to make their best pace back to camp. He also sent a mounted patrol towards Isandhlwana which reported that 'it was swarming with Zulus carrying off plunder'.

Before the infantry had come up darkness had fallen and two miles from the camp 'we formed into fighting order with the guns in the centre, flanked by a wing of the 2/24th and a native battalion with the mounted men on the extreme flanks. Little could be seen save the hill which frowned against the star-lit sky and the nek which separated it from the stony kopje on the left. On this nek we saw figures moving and as it was necessary to establish ourselves there, fire was opened with the guns and Major Wilsone Black [commanding the Mounted Infantry squadron] was ordered to move forward and occupy the kopje and, having gained it, a cheer was to be our signal to advance. The kopje was reached without opposition and we moved on. The enemy had disappeared and whether they were in the vicinity or not we could not tell. So the force was drawn up in square on the nek where we had perforce to remain until daylight.

'It was a dreadful night. All around was the reek of death and everywhere were corpses, British, colonial, Kaffir, Zulu, oxen, horses and mules, all with the bellies slit. The infantry had marched upwards of twenty-five miles that day but no one slept. Away to the west the sky was lit by flames from Rorke's Drift as the hospital burned. It seemed all too likely that there had been another disaster there.

Before it was fully light, before the full horror of the battlefield was visible, the force started marching towards the Buffalo River. In front of them was a column of smoke

121

from the Natal bank. As they marched a column of Zulus appeared on the hills on their left. Chelmsford closed up the columns but refused to halt. His troops had only the ammunition left in their pouches. A fight now could mean a defeat from lack of means to fight. The Zulus were not looking for a fight either. The two columns passed each other without a shot being fired.

As the British neared the Buffalo, the Mounted Infantry were sent on ahead. 'We feared the worst. We advanced on the river and the scouts, to the surprise of all, reported the ponts standing. The cavalry crossed below them at the shallows, as it had done twelve days before, and the first files advanced up to where the mission station had stood at the best gallop their weary and hungry horses could muster after having been under the saddle nearly thirty hours. We expected to find a repetition on a smaller scale of Isandhlwana, but as we came in sight of the commissariat stores, a cheer sounded from the top of a wall of mealie bags, from a man on the look out, and was taken up by the remainder of the little garrison, and to our delight we found there was no more bad news to be expected, at any rate for the present.'

The reek of death was no less strong here than it had been at Isandhlwana during the night. 'Hundreds of Zulus lay round the buildings and parapets in every conceivable attitude and posture. In some places they had fallen in heaps over one another—some with the most ghastly wounds from having been so close to the muzzle of the rifle which killed them; others from being consumed by fire, having fallen into the flames of the hospital as they had been killed or wounded.'

Three hundred and seventy bodies were found around the post and buried in two huge pits. Many more corpses, perhaps a hundred, had been carried away by the retreating impis and dumped into the river. For weeks afterwards, other bodies were found in the countryside where wounded warriors had crept away to die. The garrison's own losses were astonishingly light. There were fifteen dead and twelve wounded of whom two subsequently died. All but five of

122

the dead were patients in the hospital.

Chelmsford's arrival meant that the mission was safe for the time being. The garrison could relax but they could not rest. The sick and wounded needed attention and the men of both forces needed food. From a recess in the stores a cask of rum was brought out and a ration was served out. As Colour Sergeant Bourne was issuing the spirit to B Company he was astonished to see Private Hook, a lifelong teetotaller, hold out his mug for his share. 'What? You here?' 'Well' replied Hook, 'I feel I want something after that.'

Then he went back to making tea for the wounded. 'A sergeant came up and said "Lieutenant Bromhead wants you." "Wait till I put my coat on," I said. "Come as you are —straight away," he ordered, so in my shirt sleeves with my braces hanging around me, I went into the midst of the officers and Lord Chelmsford asked me all about the defence of the hospital as I was the last to leave the building. An officer took down our names and wrote down what we had done.'

Chelmsford rode on to Helpmakaar as soon as he was certain that Rorke's Drift was secure. He had hoped to find a body of survivors from Isandhlwana at the drift. Finding none he had to assume that any there were had crossed at Fugitive's Drift and made straight for the town. If they could go that way, the Zulus could have followed. The invasion of Zululand had failed. Chelmsford's immediate preoccupation must be the defence of Natal. There was no defensive force between Fugitives' Drift and Pietermaritzburg except the garrison of Helpmakaar.

As it turned out the Zulus had no intention of invading Natal and, as has been seen, Cetshwayo had specifically forbidden any move into the colony. Whatever may have been their long term intentions, they would not have taken the offensive in January before the harvest was in. Nor on 23 January were they in any mood for further fighting. Their victory at Isandhlwana had been bought at crippling cost. Their defeat at Rorke's Drift had gone far to take the edge from any elation remaining from their triumph. They had

123

destroyed a battalion of British regulars but they had learned a healthy respect for the Martini-Henry. Far from contemplating an invasion of Natal, Cetshwayo was to have trouble in reconstituting his army as many faint-hearts slipped away to help with the crops.

That the Zulus would stay on the defensive was beyond the wildest hopes of the garrison of Helpmakaar who saw themselves as the only barrier to the advance of the impis. 'We could see the watchfires of the Zulus some six miles off, and we expected them to come on and attack.' Throughout the evening the garrison had been a very makeshift affair. The little town was held, all through the evening, by such base details and convalescents as could be scraped together and armed, reinforced by the exhausted survivors of Isandhlwana, many of whom were more or less demoralized.

The two companies of the Twenty-Fourth who had been allocated to the defence of Helpmakaar had marched off under Major Spalding in the middle of the afternoon. They were going to reinforce Chard's garrison and Spalding rode ahead of them. When he was three miles from the Oscarberg he could see the road blocked by a large body of Zulus. He had met many fugitives on the road, men of Stephenson's company of NNC. They assured him that the mission had fallen. He saw a column of smoke and flames rising from the invisible buildings. Reluctantly he turned back and ordered the two companies back to Helpmakaar. Unquestionably he was right. It would have been madness for a hundred and fifty men to try and force their way through what was obviously a large enemy force just as the daylight was fading. It was not until Lord Chelmsford reached the town next morning that the garrison learned that the mission house was safe.

The mail steamer *Dunrobin Castle* was despatched from Cape Town a day ahead of her schedule to carry Chelmsford's report on Isandhlwana and Rorke's Drift. She reached cablehead in the Cape Verde Islands on Monday, 10

February and the bare bones of the story were wired to London. Late that night they were delivered to the home of the Secretary of State for the Colonies, Sir Michael Hicks Beach. The destruction of a British battalion was a disaster without parallel since the retreat from Kabul in 1841. A wave of shock and horror ran through the nation. The effect was all the greater since Britain, as usual, had been taking very little interest in South Africa. Such thoughts as could be spared from domestic events were being devoted to the war in Afghanistan.

According to the *Annual Register*, 'At the beginning of the year the mind of England had comparative rest from questions of foreign policy. The country was not prepared for any sudden developments of testing consequences and its anxieties were directed homeward, to the depression of trade and the pressure of hard times on the poor. The distress produced by the want of employment had been aggravated by a winter of great severity. All through the cold month of January, benevolence had no lack of occupation.'

The country, despite the cold and the hardships of the poor, was comfortably settled in two beliefs—in the civilizing mission of the British people and in the triumphant and irresistible march of technological progress. Of the latter there had been abundant recent evidence. In December, 1878, Joseph Wilson Swan had exhibited the first incandescent lamp at Newcastle.* Two months earlier, at Sheffield, the first floodlit football match had been played. Despite a series of bad harvests at home the price of wheat fell by almost a fifth in 1878 due to large imports from North America. Although no frozen meat was to reach Britain until 1880, the first carcasses of frozen mutton had been landed in France in 1878. The first typewriters were being imported from the United States. Although there were still ' more sailing ships on Lloyd's Register than steam, industrialization had already gone so far that William Morris, as a protest, had started producing hand-woven tapestries in 1877. Education had been made compulsory for all children

* Edison's first successful experiment was not until 21 October, 1879.

in 1870 but its effects were not yet widespread. 'On the last available statistics [for London], 2,756 men and 4,020 women signed the register by mark at their weddings.' In 1878 there were 34,007 marriages. So that more than 1 in 12 men and more than 1 in 8 women were totally illiterate. For those who could read, the *Illustrated London News* announced, four days before Rorke's Drift was attacked, 'the launching of the *Boy's Own Paper*, under the auspices of the great Tract Society. The new paper for boys begins its career with the publicly signified approval of Archbishops, Bishops, Canons, Prebendaries, Judges, Aldermen and Magistrates.' Even if the new paper was somewhat top-heavy in its patronage it probably made lighter reading than most of the books issued that year. According to statistics the leading subject category for titles published in 1879 was Theology, Sermons, Biblical &c. with 775 new titles. Educational, Classical and Philological ran second with 613, six titles ahead of Novels, Tales and Other Fiction. History and Biography came a bad fourth with 319.

Publicly the Prime Minister, Lord Beaconsfield, took an optimistic view of the country's situation. On New Year's Day he wrote to the Queen, 'The authority of Your Majesty's throne stands high again in Europe. Your Majesty's counsellors have taken a leading and successful part in the most important diplomatic meeting since the Congress of Vienna,* and Your Majesty's arms have achieved in Asia a brilliant and enduring triumph.' Privately, he was inclined to be querulous. 'You talk of my "tendency" to bronchitis! Alas! it is not a tendency: it is bronchitis absolute, and in its most aggravated form. I see people die of it every day. I don't see why I don't.' When he went to London he had to travel 'with the greatest care: in an express train and in a small saloon carriage which has been warming for me at Wycombe for a week.' An unknown lady in Lancashire had sent him as a New Year present, a pair of slippers. 'They have a coronet in the Garter on purple velvet; but so beautiful that I can never wear them, but must put them under a glass case. I

* The Congress of Berlin.

126

must forget many cares; not the least having to make a Bishop of Durham.'

The South African situation was among the least of his cares. Ever since he had come to power in 1874 he had ignored the problems of the Cape in the hope that they would solve themselves. His latest briefing had been gratifyingly emollient. On 13 January Hicks Beach had written to him that, 'There is, I hope, a good prospect of the war being successful, like the Afghan campaign.* Frere and Chelmsford seemed in the last letters I have received, very confident ... The Zulus are reported to be very much divided, and the Boers, who might place us in a very difficult position by rising in the Transvaal while we are engaged with the Zulus are said to be perfectly passive. . . . On the whole, though Frere's policy—especially in the matter of cost—is extremely inconvenient to us at the present moment, I am sanguine as to its success, and I think we shall be able, without much difficulty, to defend its main principles.'

This was just what the Prime Minister wanted to hear. It almost certainly made more impression on him than another sentence in the same letter. 'If the weakness of [Chelmsford's] forces led to any failure at first, a most serious war might result and we [the Government] should have to bear all the blame.'

The public shared Beaconsfield's lack of concern. Even the most fervent friend of oppressed races could not work up much enthusiasm for the Zulus. Stories of their atrocities, dreadful in truth and much exaggerated in the telling, had been circulating for half a century. Missionaries of all denominations had the most lurid (and most exaggerated) stories of Cetshwayo's cruelties and oppressions. The native races round the frontiers of Zululand went in terror of the impis. To those who doubted the reality of the Zulu threat, the opinion of Bishop Colenso could be quoted. On 9 January he had written to the Colonial Secretary of Natal,

* This campaign, the 2nd Afghan War, was only temporarily successful. It burst out again and in July 1880 another British battalion was lost at Maiwand.

127

'I think it right to let you know that I have reason to believe that Cetshwayo's plan is to march direct on Maritzburg and Durban, and not waste time on the country districts. This information has reached me today from native sources, and can only be relied on for what it is worth. But as I believe it to be substantially correct, I think it is my duty to report it.' If Colenso, the friend and protector of the Zulus, believed that Cetshwayo was aiming for Durban, as his ancestors had done twice before, it was hard to depict the Zulus as an oppressed minority.

In Britain the general view was that there was no alternative to fighting the Zulus sooner or later and, if it had to be done, it should be done quickly and efficiently. As one paper wrote, 'The situation may not involve the interests of Empire, but, at least, it may necessitate considerable political embarrassment and great expense.'

The news of the Isandhlwana disaster was consequently a shattering blow. A fashionable boot maker remarked to an officer ordered out to Zululand, 'Very sad business, sir—nothing like it in England since I can remember. We lost three customers by it.' The Prime Minister confessed, 'I am greatly stricken; and have to support others, which increases the burden; almost intolerable.' To the Queen he wrote on 11 February, 'It has been a very agitating day with this terrible news from S. Africa, which to Lord Beaconsfield is very unintelligible. The cabinet met, and sent five regiments of infantry instead of three asked for by Lord Chelmsford, and all the cavalry, and artillery, and stores which he requested. It is to be hoped that he may be equal to the occasion, but it is impossible to feel that this disaster has occurred to the Headquarters Column, which he was commanding himself.'

Faced with the results of his own neglect and inattention, Beaconsfield was looking for a scapegoat. Chelmsford was the obvious man for the role particularly as the Prime Minister could count on the support of that part of the army which looked to Wolseley for leadership. Sir Garnet was anxious that the blame should be diverted from those responsible for the recent army reforms. There had been many who had been forecasting that only disaster could result from trusting to an army 'composed of young generals and boy soldiers'. He made no secret of his opinion. 'It is no question of young soldiers, but of bad leading. Had a man like Evelyn Wood been in command, or a man like Colonel Colley, or many others I could name, the war would have been over. Such men make mistakes, but their very mistakes are better than the plans of unknown officers who command no respect or want the confidence of those under them.' Lord Chelmsford was not an unknown officer and he was greatly loved and trusted by his men but he was not an unqualified admirer of Sir Garnet Wolseley. This kind of support was exactly what the Prime Minister needed.

Unfortunately for him, he was not allowed to use it. Immediately the news arrived the Queen telegraphed to Lord Chelmsford that 'Her Majesty places entire confidence in you'. The Commander-in-Chief followed this with a message that he was 'satisfied that you have done and will continue to do everything that is right'. Faced with these two royal and published telegrams, it was impossible for the Government to place the blame on the commander on the spot. They set in motion, with the enthusiastic support of Wolseley, a sustained campaign of denigration which lasted for decades but they had to find something else to divert public attention from their shortcomings. The defence of Rorke's Drift suited their purpose splendidly.

In his telegraphed report, necessarily short, Chelmsford had written that 'Rorke's Drift for twelve hours had been attacked by 3,000 to 4,000 Zulus. The defence by some eighty men of the 24th, under Bromhead, and a few others, most gallant. Lieutenant Chard, R.E. senior officer. 370 bodies lay close around the post,' Beaconsfield seized on this opening. On 13 February in the House of Lords he refused to comment on the general situation of the war but declared 'We must not forget the exhibition of heroic valour on the part of those who have been spared; and the heroism of those eighty men who for twelve hours kept back 4,000

129

of the enemy and in the end repulsed them, shows that the stamina of the English soldiers has not diminished.'

The tribute was well deserved but the intention behind it was the classic conjurer's misdirection. The government had neglected South Africa. They had devised, as a method of saving trouble and expense, a politicians' scheme for federating two colonies and two independent republics. The plan was tidy but had no connection with reality. They sent out a distinguished pro-consul of known forcefulness to arrange things. Then they put the whole business out of their minds. When, inevitably, the scheme resulted in serious trouble, all the Government could do was to send out reinforcements they had previously refused and try to focus public attention on something else. They were fortunate that they had such a shining example of courage and steadfastness ready to hand.

Eleven of Chard's garrison were awarded the Victoria Cross, making it the most highly decorated battle in British history. This unprecedented largesse was well spread out to make the maximum public impact. The *London Gazette* of 2 May announced awards to Chard, to Bromhead and to six other members of B Company. Six weeks later Surgeon-Major Reynolds was decorated. It was not until 18 November that the *Gazette* carried the award of a cross to Assistant Commissary Dalton and another was announced a fortnight later to Corporal Schiess of the Natal Native Contingent. Colour-Sergeant Bourne and a corporal of the Commissariat Department were given the Distinguished Conduct Medal.

Meanwhile Chard and Bromhead were given accelerated promotion. Bromhead would have succeeded in any case to one of five captaincies made vacant by the losses at Isandhlwana. He was given a majority by brevet immediately. Chard, deservedly, received an even more unusual rise. He was given a supernumerary captaincy in the Royal Engineers and, dated from 23 January, a brevet majority. He thus became the first man in history to move from a lieutenancy to a majority in the army (but not in his corps) in a single day. The Reverend Mr Smith was given a regular commission as a chaplain and eventually Colour-Sergeant Bourne was commissioned. The House of Commons voted thanks to both Chard and Bromhead.

The Queen commissioned Lady Butler to paint a picture commemorating the defence and the army made many of the participants available to the artist so that she could paint them from life. In 1881 the Queen was shown the Queen's Colour of the Twenty-Fourth which was recovered from the Buffalo River. She attached to it a wreath of *immortelles* and directed that in future the staff of that Colour in both battalions should carry a silver wreath 'to commemorate the devotion displayed by Lieutenants Melvill and Coghill in their heroic endeavour to save the Colour on 22 January 1879, and of the noble defence of Rorke's Drift.' She also, at different times received Chard and Bromhead, the former being invited to a weekend at Balmoral and presented with a diamond ring.

Chard's greatest day after his return to England must have been when he was presented with 'a sword and chronometer by his fellow townsmen at Plymouth. The sword has been specially manufactured by Messrs Hunt and Roskell. The scabbard, of silver, is ornamented in panels of *repoussé*, representing—1, the mission house at Rorke's Drift; 2, shields bearing the arms of Plymouth and England; 3, 'Vulcan forging the arms of Achilles', in allusion to the generally defensive character of the operations of the Royal Engineers; 4, a trophy of broken Zulu weapons; 5, an allegorical device of lion and elephant, symbolizing the pursuit and defeat of the enemy, and the triumph of British arms in Africa. The opposite side has corresponding panels showing—1, the Victoria Cross; 2, shields with the arms of Major Chard and the Royal Engineers; 3, Britannia; 4, trophy of Engineers' tools crowned with laurel by Fame; 5, St George of England vanquishing the dragon. The guard is of silver, pierced and richly carved with the rose, shamrock and thistle, surrounded by oak leaves. The blade, of the finest tempered steel, bears on one side the motto, "Strong to defend the right—Swift to avenge the wrong," and on the other a record of the presentation of the sword "in recognition of his gallant defence of Rorke's Drift."'

Although there were other setbacks in Zululand before Chelmsford achieved the decisive battle he sought at Ulundi, five months after Rorke's Drift, the public continued, as the government had intended, to take little interest in the army. When the Army Estimates came before the House of Commons in March, 1879, the *Illustrated London News* commented that 'One might have imagined that the estimates for the present year would have attracted special Parliamentary attention. It has not proved so. They cannot successfully compete with those habits of members which are best indicated by the words "dinner hour". Colonel Stanley, the Secretary of State, was unable to get into committee until seven o'clock and was therefore subject to the disadvantage of explaining the estimates to a comparatively empty house.'

The defence of Rorke's Drift was a triumph of skill, discipline, courage and stamina but it was a very small triumph. A hundred well-armed men with unlimited ammunition and a good position held off for twelve hours a magnificently brave horde who were effectively without firearms. In any other of Britain's endemic colonial wars of the nineteeth century it would scarcely have been noticed. It would have received a glowing mention in the regimental history and been forgotten elsewhere. A centuries old tradition laid down that this was the kind of thing that the British infantryman was expected to do.

The Zulu onslaught must have been terrifying to see and hear but, statistically speaking, it was not very dangerous to men behind even improvized fortifications. Of the fit men of B Company only six were serious casualties, and one of them, Private Cole, died only because his nerve broke and he ran out of the protection of the ramparts. This was not a heavy loss for twelve hours of heavy fighting.

Rorke's Drift became a legend because it was juxtaposed with Isandhlwana. Beaconsfield, with his showman's instinct, built it up to epic proportions because it suited his policy to do so. This was not the only cause. It restored the public's

13. 1373 Private Alfred Henry Hook, VC, one of the men who helped evacuate patients from the hospital while under attack

14. 593 Private William Jones, VC; he, like Hook, held off Zulu assaults on the hospital while the wounded were moved to safety

15. 1240 Corporal William Allan, VC

16. The investiture of Major Chard with the Victoria Cross

confidence in the advance of technology. They had been conditioned to believe that scientific progress gave Britain an automatic superiority over the more primitive races of Africa. As usual public expectations of what technology could achieve outran the facts. It was imagined that the Martini-Henry gave an absolute superiority over Zulus armed with stabbing weapons. In fact the Martini, being a single loading weapon, gave only a limited advantage. As long as the soldier had to fumble in his pouch for each round, he could not fire fast enough to keep off overwhelming numbers in close formation and willing to accept vast casualties, unless he was in close formation and given all-round protection by the fire of his comrades. At Isandhlwana, Pulleine's men were drawn, by Durnford's folly and insubordination, into fighting with their flanks in the air and their rear open. They fought beyond the capability of their weapons.

Rorke's Drift showed the Martini-Henry at its best. Thanks to the foresight of Dalton and Chard the battle was fought under ideal conditions with a maximum of protection for the men and unlimited ammunition within a few yards. Moreover, since for most of the battle the riflemen's positions were static they could lay out their rounds of ammunition beside them rather than having to find each round in their pouch.

It may be that the defenders of the mission station got more acclamation than would normally have come to them. It cannot be said that they got more than they deserved. They behaved according to a great tradition which once made a French marshal remark, 'The British infantry are the finest in the world. Fortunately there are not many of them.' The Twenty-Fourth were not present at Waterloo, but Rorke's Drift shows that they would have been worthy of Wellington's highest praise after that battle, 'I never saw the British infantry behave so well.'

Appendix

Victoria Crosses at Rorke's Drift

Royal Engineers:
    Lieutenant John Rouse Merriott Chard.

Twenty-Fourth (2nd Warwickshire) Foot:
    Lieutenant Gonville Bromhead.
    1240 Corporal Allan, William.
    1362 Private Hitch, Frederick.
    1373 Private Hook, Alfred Henry.
     716 Private Jones, Robert.
     593 Private Jones, William.
    1393 Private Williams, John.

Commissariat Department:
    Assistant Commissary James Langley Dalton.

Army Hospital Corps:
    Surgeon-Major James Henry Reynolds,
        M.B. M.Ch (Durham).

Natal Native Contingent:
    Corporal Schiess, Friedrich Carl.

Principal Sources

There are four main accounts of the defence of Rorke's Drift. These are Chard's report to Lord Chelmsford, (published in the Royal Engineer's Journal for August, 1879) Surgeon-Major Reynold's report (in the Report of the Army Hospitals Department for 1878 [sic]), a later account by Chaplain Smith which can be found in the *Historical Records of the 24th Regiment* (see below) and the description by Private Henry Hook. The latter was taken down by some other person and I do not know where the original is to be found. Most of Hook's account is reproduced in the Royal Magazine for 1905 but other parts, clearly from the same source, are to be found in Hook's obituary in the *Daily News* for 14 March, 1905. Private Lugg of the Twenty-Fourth also sent two letters which were published in the Bristol Observer. The most important of the other works consulted for this book are:

Jack Adams, *The South Wales Borderers*, 1968

Walter Asche & E. V. Wyatt Edgell, *Story of the Zulu Campaign*, 1880

Robert Biddulph, *Lord Cardwell at the War Office*, 1904

C. T. Binns, *The Last Zulu King, The Life & Death of Cetshwayo*, 1955

Brian Bond, *The Effect of the Cardwell Reforms. Journal of Royal United Service Institution*, November 1960

G. E. Buckle, *Life of Benjamin Disraeli, Lord Beaconsfield*, Vol vi, 1920

Reginald Coupland, *Zulu Battle Piece—Isandhlwana*, 1948

Benjamin Disraeli, *Letters to Lady Bradford and Lady Chesterfield*, (Lord Zetland Ed) 1929

A. W. Durnford, *A Soldier's Life & Work in South Africa*, 1882

R. C. K. Ensor, *England 1870–1914*, 1936

Gerald French, *Lord Chelmsford—the Zulu War*, 1939

H. Rider Haggard, *Cetshwayo and his white neighbours*, 1882

H. Rider Haggard, *The Days of my Life, 1926*

G. Hamilton Browne, *A Lost Legionary in South Africa*, 1880

A. A. Hardinge, *The Fourth Earl of Carnarvon*, 1925

Christopher Hibbert, *The Destruction of Lord Raglan*, 1961

Victoria Hicks Beach, *Sir Michael Hicks Beach, Lord St Aldwyn*, 1932

Peter Hinchcliffe, *John William Colenso*, 1964

F. W. D. Jackson, *Isandhlwana—The Sources Re-examined*, Journal of the Society for Army Historical Research 1965 (Nos 173, 175 & 176)

Joseph Lehmann, *All Sir Garnet*, 1964

J. P. Mackinnon & Sydney Shadbolt, *The South African Campaign of 1879*, 1880

John Martineau, *Life & Correspondence of Sir Bartle Frere*, 1895

Frederick Maurice and George Arthur, *Life of Lord Wolseley*, 1924

W. E. Montague, *Campaigning in South Africa*, 1880

Donald R. Morris, *The Washing of the Spears*, 1965

Frederick Myatt, *The March to Magdala*, 1970

Narrative of the Field Operations Connected with the Zulu War, prepared by the Intelligence Branch, 1881

The Panmure Papers, (George Douglas Ed) 1908

H. Hallam Parr, *A Sketch of the Kaffir and Zulu Wars*, 1880

George Paton, Farquar Glennie & William Penn Symons, *Historical Records of the 24th Regiment*, 1892

Oliver Rainsford, *The Great Trek*

E. A. Ritter, *Shaka Zulu, The Rise of the Zulu Kingdom*, 1955

Horace Smith Dorrien, *Memories of Forty-Eight Years Service*, 1925

Lord Stanmore, *Life of Lord Herbert of Lea*, 1906

G. Tylden, *The Principal Small Arms Carried by the British Army, Journal of the Society of Army Historical Research*, 1967, No 184

Willoughby Verner, *Military Life of HRH the Duke of Cambridge*, 1905

Letters of Queen Victoria (2nd Series) (G. E. Buckle Ed), 1928

F. E. Whitton, *Rorke's Drift, Blackwood's Magazine*, February, 1934

Owen Wheeler, *The War Office, Past & Present*, 1914

Monica Wilson & Leonard Thompson, *Oxford History of South Africa*, 1969/71

Lord Wolseley, *The Soldier's Pocket Book* (5th edition), 1886

Evelyn Wood, *From Midshipman to Field Marshal*, 1906

Basil Worsfold, *Sir Bartle Frere. A Footnote to the history of the British Empire*, 1923

The Times

The Illustrated London News

The London Gazette

The Annual Register

The Bristol Observer

Royal Engineers Journal for December, 1897 & June, 1960

The Sapper for August, 1963

Index

142

143

* Hook, Pte Henry, 24th Foot: See p. 138 (Churcham, Glos.) ref. in Arthur Mee's GLOUCESTERSHIRE (The Kings England) (1938 edition, 1950 reprint). (Gives details of Hook's birthplace and burial).

* Pte John Williams, 24th Foot: See page 79 (Llantarnam) ref. in Arthur Mee's <u>Monthmouthshire</u> (The King's England) for burial place of Pte Williams + a note on Rorke's Drift, pp 79–80. (First published, Feb. 1951)

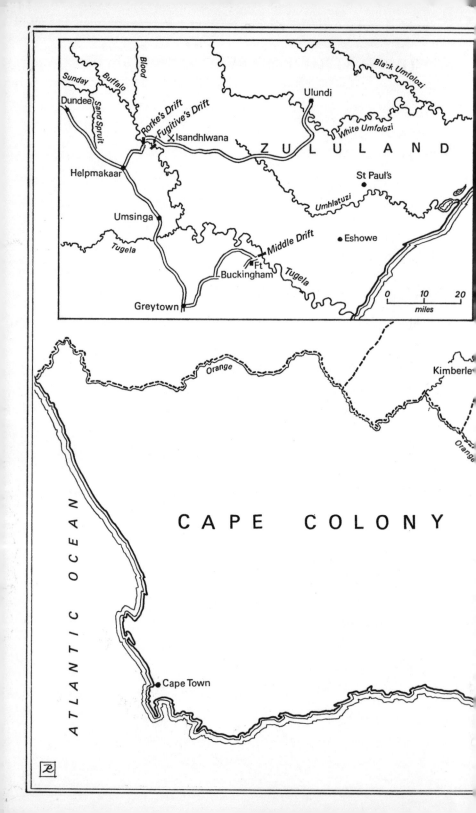